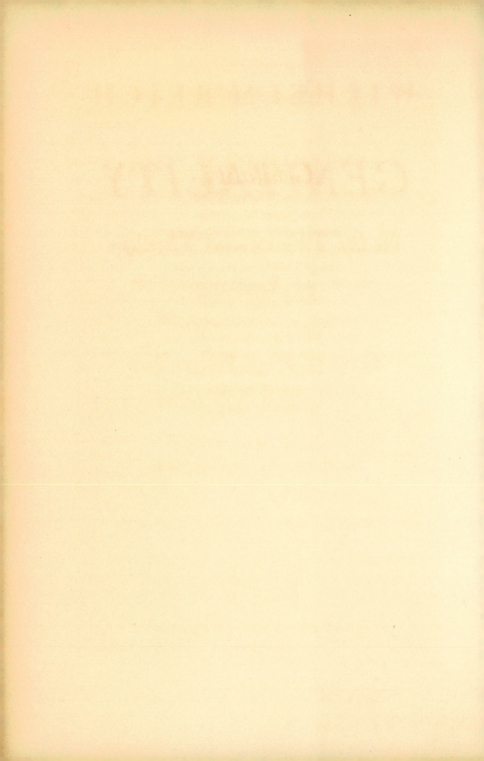

Genitality

WILHELM REICH

GENITALITY

In the Theory and Therapy
of Neurosis

Early Writings, Volume Two

TRANSLATED FROM THE GERMAN
BY PHILIP SCHMITZ

EDITED BY MARY HIGGINS
AND CHESTER M. RAPHAEL, M.D.

FARRAR STRAUS GIROUX
New York

Published simultaneously in Canada by McGraw-Hill Ryerson Ltd., Toronto
Printed in the United States of America
First printing, 1980

Library of Congress Cataloging in Publication Data
Reich, Wilhelm, 1897–1957.
Genitality in the theory and therapy of neurosis.
Translation of Die Funktion des Orgasmus.
Includes bibliographical references and index.
1. Neuroses. 2. Sex (Psychology) 3. Sexual disorders. 4. Orgasm.
I. Higgins, Mary. II. Raphael, Chester M. III. Title.
[DNLM: 1. Neuroses. 2. Orgasm. HQ21 R347f]
RC530.R4413   1979   616.8'914   79–18720

Love, work and knowledge are the well-springs of our life. They should also govern it.

WILHELM REICH

Contents

Editors' Preface

Why do neurotic symptoms disappear when a patient experiences genital satisfaction? And why do they reappear when the sexual need-tension builds up again? Does the genital orgasm have a biological function irrespective of procreation? If so, what is that function? And what is its significance for the theory and therapy of neurosis?

These are questions to which Reich addressed himself more than fifty years ago. The results of his investigation were first published in 1927 by the International Psychoanalytic Press under the title *Die Funktion des Orgasmus*. Reich considered this study, which he dedicated to his teacher Freud, to be within the framework of psychoanalytic thought. However, the coolness of Freud, who had turned increasingly from a biological to a psychological orientation, and the growing hostility of his colleagues, whose primary interest lay in the psychology of the neurosis rather than in its biological basis, soon corrected that view. The book was never republished or translated.

Later, in 1942, Reich published a scientific autobiography under the same title, *The Function of the Orgasm*. With the exception of a detailed description of the orgasm process, however, no part of the 1927 volume was included. In reusing the title of the earlier book, he wished, it is apparent, to accentuate the fact that the whole development of his work flowed out of his orgasm research and his conviction that the orgasm function holds the key to the most basic questions in nature.

We are now presenting for the first time a second, re-vised edition of the 1927 publication under the new title *Genitality in the Theory and Therapy of Neurosis.* This title change has been made in order to avoid any possible confusion with the 1942 work, which is widely distributed throughout the world.

All the other revisions—additions, deletions, word and chapter-title changes—were made by Reich himself be-tween 1937 and 1945. Often, they reflect his separation from Freud and psychoanalysis and his recognition that this investigation of genitality derived from his own com-mitment to a search for the source of the energy which precipitates and sustains the neurosis rather than from Freudian theory or practice. It is of interest to note that he has reversed the position of the first two chapters. In 1927, he began with a presentation of the neurotic conflict as it was understood by Freud. In this second edition, the in-itial focus is placed on the natural function of orgastic potency, the core of Reich's orgasm theory.

Aside from his independent position, Reich's changes mirror the development of his experimental research in Norway (1935–9) which confirmed the validity of the orgasm formula and revealed the existence of a demon-strable biological energy to which he gave the name "orgone." Material that was still hypothetical in 1927 is now clarified authoritatively from the perspective of his knowledge of this physical energy.

Of all the bodily functions, it is the genital function that is most subject to interference by social restrictions. It is difficult to make clear its significance, not because the function itself is complicated, but because it is an awkward subject tainted with lascivious thinking and guilt. In the practice of medicine it is either avoided or, as in the sex therapies that have become so popular recently, it is viewed as a purely local phenomenon. Reich's discovery of the unifying, energy-regulating function of the genital orgasm is still not understood, but today, when many of the moral dams against genitality have been removed and society is flooded with the evidence of unsatisfied genital longing—pornography, teenage violence and suicide, wanton murder, child abuse, etc.—it becomes an essential guidepost to clarity and, hopefully, to the eventual prevention of the neuroses and functional diseases which now exist *en masse*.

Mary Higgins, Trustee
The Wilhelm Reich Infant Trust Fund

Chester M. Raphael, M.D.

Forest Hills, N.Y.
1979

Genitality

Foreword
to the
First Edition

The theoretical questions dealt with here arose out of certain practical issues in the psychoanalytic treatment of emotionally ill persons. I had been struck by the connection between the positive as well as the negative therapeutic reactions of these patients and their genitality; I discussed some aspects of this in the *International Journal for Psychoanalysis*.[1] Pursuing the theoretical questions further, I was able to regularly establish causal connections between the neurotic processes and disturbances of genital functioning which explain the therapeutic reactions. These connections permit us to understand why impotence, or, as the case may be, frigidity, is a regular concomitant of neurosis, and also why the form of the neurosis determines the form of the disturbance of genital functioning and vice versa. Seen in relation to the function of the orgasm, which gradually assumed a central posi-

[1] "Über Spezifität der Onanieformen," Bd. VIII, 1922 ["Concerning Specific Forms of Masturbation," *Early Writings*, Vol. I (New York: Farrar, Straus and Giroux, 1975)]; "Über Genitalität vom Standpunkt der psychoanalytischen Prognose und Therapie," Bd. X, 1924 ["On Genitality: From the Standpoint of Psychoanalytic Prognosis and Therapy," *ibid.*]; "Weitere Bemerkungen über die therapeutische Bedeutung der Genitallibido," Bd. XI, 1925 ["Further Remarks on the Therapeutic Significance of Genital Libido," *ibid.*]; "Über die Quellen der neurotischen Angst (Beitrag zur Theorie der psychoanalytischen Therapie)," Bd. XII, 1926 ["On the Sources of Neurotic Anxiety (A Contribution to the Theory of Psychoanalytic Therapy)"].

tion, the problem of anxiety, certain marital and social phenomena, as well as the issue of the therapy of neurosis, also appear in a clearer light. Although this work builds entirely on Freud's theories of sexuality and of neurosis, I cannot presume that the concept of the dynamics of psychoanalytic therapy and its tasks set forth here have been accepted by the Freudian school; what follows reflects my own clinical experience. Nevertheless, I believe that my view of the importance of genitality, particularly the genital orgasm, to the theory and therapy of neuroses and of the neurotic character, is a direct continuation of fundamental psychoanalytic theory and makes possible a more consistent application of the theory of neurosis to therapy.

Many questions relating to the theory of character formation and ego psychology are also intimately connected with the problem of the orgasm. I have attempted as far as possible to exclude them from discussion so as not to disrupt the unity of the subject. Furthermore, the peculiar difficulties associated with the psychoanalytic theory of character formation made their exclusion necessary. In the first place, the clinical basis of the theory is not yet sufficiently complete and, second, the psychoanalytic theory of character formation, systematically laid out in Freud's *The Ego and the Id*, would have had to have been dealt with in detail from the perspective of sexual theory. I feel it necessary to state this, lest I be reproached for having neglected ego psychology.

However, the exclusion of this major theme, which I attempted to outline under the title "Drive Psychology and the Theory of Character" in a course given at the Vienna Psychoanalytic Institute and which I shall reserve for separate treatment, created serious gaps in the present work that could give rise to some misunderstanding. In dealing with the theory of sexuality, I have striven for completeness to the extent my experience permitted. Where it is limited, as, for example, with regard to the disturbances of genital functioning in satyriasis, epilepsy, and the psychoses, I have, despite isolated findings, omitted discussion. Insofar as any misunderstandings may involve factual matters, I hope to be able to dispel them later.

I publish this work fully aware that it deals with very "explosive material" and that I must therefore be prepared for emotionally-based objections. It is not easy to impersonally and unemotionally discuss the orgasm and its role in the life of the individual and in society. The subject is too much a part of everyone's experience and, consequently, there is always the danger of distortion or ideological coloring of factual judgment. The question, however, is not the presence or absence of an ideology but rather the type of ideology involved; that is, whether an ethically evaluative attitude toward the problem of sex leads one away from the truth or whether a different moral attitude compels one to pursue it. Moreover, there is an essential difference between measuring the facts of sexual life according to the arbitrary yardstick of some unverifiable "good" or "bad" and assessing them on the basis of a nonethical objective, noting, for instance, whether a given behavior benefits or harms an individual's psychic health, that is, his ability to love and to work. I believe I have adhered to the latter type of evaluation in dealing with issues of sexuality in marriage and the prevailing sexual morality.

Since to the best of my knowledge no investigation such as this one has ever before been attempted—indeed, the function of the orgasm appears to be the stepchild of both psychology and physiology—it is to be hoped that the results themselves will justify the undertaking and that factual criticism alone will assess the importance of its subject matter. The facts themselves protect against the danger of exaggeration; the raw statistics regarding the frequency of impotence and frigidity among neurotics and the few detailed case histories can reflect only imperfectly the impression gained by the practicing physician, unless he is determined to close his mind to it at any price. Moreover, at present there is a much greater likelihood that the importance of the sexual function will be underestimated rather than overestimated, a fact far more harmful than if the reverse were to be the case. This would seem to account for the inaccessibility of the somatic foundation of neurosis, insofar as it was approached at all. However, a more accurate explanation reveals that, except in psychoanalysis, inquiries about the sexual life of the "nervous" patient are still anxiously avoided. It is historically interesting that while the physiologists spoke out against the psychogenetic theory of neurosis and searched in vain for a somatic basis, it was the medical psychologist Freud, using a psychological method, who discovered the "somatic core of neurosis." Thirty years of psychoanalytic experience separates that discovery and the present. Our examination of the function of the orgasm, which is a psychophysical phenomenon, must therefore reach far back, taking as its starting point the psychic manifestations of somatic disturbances in sexual functioning subsumed by Freud under the term "actual neuroses" and contrasted with the "psychoneuroses." As a result of the rapid progress psychoanalysis has made in fathoming the psychic causes of neurosis, there has been a waning of interest in the "libido stasis" originally thought of as somatic in nature.[2] The concept of libido increasingly acquired the meaning of a psychic rather than a physical energy. Interest in the "actual neurotic (i.e., somatic) core of neurosis" suffered unwarrantably from this shift. In the past ten years it has scarcely been mentioned. Freud himself still holds fast to the theory of actual neurosis,[3] although since 1924 he has not dealt any further with this aspect of neurosis.

A study of the causes, manifestations, and effects of somatic libido stasis, extending without interruption over several years, has convinced me that Freud's theory of actual neurosis, a theory that has withstood many objections on the part of psychoanalysts themselves, not only is heuristically useful but, as a theory for the physiological basis of neurosis, also forms an indispensable part of psychopathology and the theory of analytic therapy. Thus, this work has an additional purpose, namely, to remind us that Freud has shown us a path along which we may approach the organic basis of neurosis, and to demonstrate that we can effectively utilize his long-neglected discovery in both practice and theory.

1926   Wilhelm Reich

---

[2] In the Freudian definition, libido stasis signified an accumulation of physiochemical sexual substance that created physical tensions and manifested itself as an instinctual urge to sexual satisfaction *(Three Contributions to the Theory of Sex)*. "The neuroses that can be derived only from disturbances of sexual life show the greatest clinical similarity to the phenomena of intoxication and abstinence that arise from the habitual use of toxic, pleasure-producing substances" *(ibid.,* p. 216).

[3] "Contemporary Medicine in Self-portraits" ("Die Medizin der Gegenwart in Selbstdarstellungen," 1924.)

Foreword
to the
Second Edition

Eighteen years have passed since the writing of this book. Much has changed in that time. The face of the world has altered and, consequently, so has that of science. Psychoanalysis has also been affected. I have come to this assessment with the most profound regret. In the years between 1921 and 1926 I was collecting the material for the first edition of this work, and in spite of its novelty, I thought of myself as a sincere and unhesitating champion of psychoanalysis. At that time psychoanalysis was still in sharp opposition to a world that resisted it and to official science that derided it. The arduous pioneering efforts on behalf of Freud's work in which I had engaged even as a young student (from 1919 on) prove that I felt in agreement with Freud's doctrines. Although there were many misgivings and uncertainties, *the struggle to bring about the acceptance of the sexual etiology of neuroses* obscured the initial faint doubts concerning the scientific conclusiveness of the prevailing battle over Freud's teachings. People whose contact with the psychoanalytic movement came later no longer encountered this condition of struggle, out of which total identification with, and an utter dedication to, psychoanalysis inevitably grew. I think back with pleasure and pride to that time, in spite of everything that has happened since.

As a result of certain objections raised by my opponents in the thick of this struggle, I became convinced that the enduring, indestructible core of psychoanalysis is its sexual theory, just because it was and still is the issue of the doctrine most fiercely attacked. Coming to Freud from sexology and biology, I perhaps felt the lack of a fundamental theory of the biological basis of neurosis more acutely than did my colleagues who came from internal medicine or from materialistic philosophy. Thus, although when I first encountered Freud's teachings, his view of "actual neurosis" seemed completely unclear, I nevertheless felt it was *the* pivotal point from which the natural scientific study of sexual biology had to proceed. The foreword to the first edition of this work bears clear witness to my basic attitude at that time.

The theory of actual neurosis, the oldest of Freud's concepts, was only loosely connected, as though by chance and not necessity, to the body of his psychological system. I very soon noticed that, even within the psychoanalytic camp, this theory met with little understanding and much enmity. Freud himself continued to defend it for some years without, however, devoting himself to it more specifically. Later, he seemed to be moving away from it, when he wanted to have anxiety considered as the sole cause of repression and no longer, as he had earlier, as its consequence as well.

A clinical accident in the second year of my psychoanalytic practice put the solution of a problematic detail into my hands from which all my later independent work originated. A severely neurotic man whom I was unable to reach with my psychoanalytic interpretations was temporarily relieved of his symptoms whenever, as it were fortuitously, he succeeded in achieving orgastic satisfaction. Nor was this a case of pure actual neurosis; rather, it was a complicated case of compulsion neurosis. From then on I began to observe my patients closely with regard to their genital behavior, and so gained knowledge of the pathological material dealt with in this book. Gradually I developed my views on the function of the orgasm within the framework of the then prevailing psychoanalytic theory of neurosis. These views not only fit well into the theory; they in fact actually supplemented important parts of it. Above all, they opened up as-yet-unexplored perspectives for understanding the biological basis of neurosis. My attitude to my discovery was entirely innocent and unsuspecting. I presented it to my professional organization as an integral contribution to the psychoanalytic theory of neurosis. Very soon, however, I noticed that my discovery gave offense. Colleagues who previously had acknowledged and praised my work were becoming irritated and "critical." When I presented the subject for the first time, in the autumn of 1923, my fellow professionals countered with innumerable cases of patients who, while indeed markedly neurotic, were nevertheless genitally "fully potent." Although today this sounds unbelievable, it is a fact. One of these psychoanalysts is still repeating such unfounded arguments. Even Freud was noticeably cool to the introduction of the orgasm issue into psychoanalysis. At one session he claimed that there was very often nothing wrong with homosexuals genitally. Thus I found myself obliged, even for the first edition of this book, to make it clear in the foreword that my views were "not as yet accepted by psychoanalysis." It is important to mention these ancient matters because with time the orgasm theory became part and parcel of psychoanalysis without its true significance ever having been understood. Even less were, or are, psychoanalysts ready to confront the ramifications of this theory. But it is out of this theory that those methods and conclusions which have brought me into serious conflict with the official position of psychoanalysis have gradually evolved: the sexual economy of psychic life; the technique of character analysis; my views on infantile and pubertal genital functioning; my critique of the ruinous sexual regulation of our society; and, above all, the clinical criticism of the direction in which psychoanalysis has developed since the hypothesis of the "death instinct" was adopted. The orgasm theory leads quite logically into the fields of physiology and biology, and to experiments on the vegetative nervous system. Sex economy and psychoanalysis are today totally separate disciplines, both in method and content; they have only their historical origins in common. Views on the economy of neurosis have become just as divergent as those on sexuality and anxiety. Sex economy is not a psychology; rather, it is a biophysical theory of sexuality.

Since the psychoanalytic community has preferred not to be identified with my findings and views, it seems only proper to forbid representatives of psychoanalysis from claiming my theory as part of their discipline. People who refuse to accept the core and consequences of a discovery have no claim on the fruits of work done by others. I prefer to bring righteous enmity upon myself rather than burden myself with questionable friendship. If for years, and to its later detriment, I represented the orgasm theory as part of psychoanalysis, I did so in good faith. But when members of the psychoanalytic community lay claim to the orgasm theory, yet avoid the term "sex economy," they are acting perniciously. No realistic friendship can withstand this. However, in practice, it is probably always impossible to protect one's intellectual property against pillage. Intellectual work is valued far too little, despite all the hypocritical reverence paid to intelligence.

From the very outset, investigation of the phenomenon "orgasm" encountered a series of difficulties. Having always been a stepchild among the disciplines of natural science, no area is as obscure as this. The years of research that followed the completion of this book have taught me that my first formulations, although they had gone a long way toward dealing with the problems then at hand, had neither done justice to the scope of the theme nor grasped the core of the issue. It would serve no purpose to blame the generally prevailing sexual reticence and timidity, although they undoubtedly had an inhibitory effect on the study of the orgasm. I have recently come to believe that there is another reason for the difficulties I experienced: the fragmentation of natural science into a great number of narrow fields, each evolving special methods of research. The researchers in each field are so intimately involved with their own particular questions and methods that, even with the best intentions, they can scarcely understand each other. Thus a natural-philosophical synthesis of the scientific knowledge mankind has acquired about the life processes would have a far harder time today than in the past, when as little was known about electronics and the quantum theory as about the theory of relativity, unconscious psychic life, or the hydration theory of life. Nowadays the nature of the atom can be explored without knowledge of the psychology of the unconscious; in turn, research in psychology can be pursued without any knowledge of the vegetative streaming of the organism. The delimitation of a field, its relative independence, guarantees the respective researchers great freedom within their own realms. It is different in fields in which artificially separated areas of the life process either overlap or merge. They are nodal points of different scientific approaches. If sex-economic research was widely accused of a lack of modesty and an unwillingness to set itself limits, this lay in the fact that its critics were measuring it with the same yardsticks as those applied to the prevailing professional disciplines. The trouble lay not in a presumptuousness on the part of the sex economists but in the nature of the realm in which they were working and in a new principle that they were forced to apply to the scientific investigation of sexuality—that every phase of the life process is simultaneously the object of some specialized science *and* of sexological research. Sexual anatomy is distinct from sexual physiology, which, in turn, is distinct from sexual psychology and sexual biology. In the past few years sexual sociology has arisen and has similarly claimed the right to a separate existence. A bit much all at once, to be sure! And confusing in the fullest sense of the word! Even now sexology does not, like physiology or psychology, for instance, represent a unified area of research with its own lines of demarcation. This is because with the fragmenting of the science of life into the life sciences, the study of sexuality was itself dispersed into separate specialties. The sexual function is the core of the life function per se. Dividing sexology into separate disciplines had some great advantages but also very grave disadvantages. One of the advantages was that specialized methods made it possible to achieve a far-reaching understanding of the "various facets" of the sexual process, such as reproduction, copulation, excitation of the sexual organs, psychic phenomena, dynamics, and so forth. The disadvantage, however, lay in the fact that every specialized sexological investigation remained trapped in details, unable to penetrate to the basic principle of sexuality. Students of reproduction, with their particular methods, were unable to grasp the tension-charge process, for instance, which is one of the basic principles governing sexuality. Psychoanalysts were able to comprehend the psychic process of the unconscious, and even to underpin it with a dynamic principle, libido, but had to admit that they could not affirm the nature of the tension-relaxation mechanism which governs psychic functioning. In fact, psychoanalysts betrayed a remarkable—and perhaps, for their own field, advantageous—reluctance to occupy themselves with physiological questions. Such attempts as were made failed because psychic concepts and ideas were carried into the physiological realm, and organic issues were "interpreted"—cautiously by Ferenczi and mystically by Groddeck, for example. That psychoanalysts strove to penetrate an area reflected over and over again in the psyche is understandable, but they were never successful. And indeed, after spending twenty-three years investigating the orgasm, I must say that it is not the failure of their attempts but rather the success of my own undertaking that seems incredible, since the path to the methodologically correct understanding of the central issue of sexuality was so thoroughly hidden.

Let us return to the disadvantages inherent in the compartmentalization of sexology. If, say, an investigator ascertains the functions of internal secretions, it becomes extremely tempting to attribute related issues in the everyday sexual behavior of living creatures to internal secretion; to explain impotence, for instance, as a disturbance of internal secretion. Or, say, another investigator has discovered a center in the brain the destruction of which produces alterations in sexual functioning. Immediately this center is made responsible for *all* sexual transgressions. While this foreword was being written, sensational news came from Vienna that "an organ producing the internal secretion for chastity" had been discovered (supposedly it was the pineal gland which worked against the gonads) and theology could rejoice. In no other field was, and is, scientific caution, which is generally so heavily stressed, sidestepped as often as in the field of sexology. This, too, is understandable. In no other field is the hope for scientific solutions so urgent, because no other is of such burning concern for everybody or so preempted by metaphysics and religion. Presumably, ethics will be able to act as the custodian of sexuality only so long as sexology is fragmented among scientific specialties which, having been unable to discover the basic principle of sexuality, remain free to make the leap into ethical metaphysics. From among the innumerable examples of this transilience to be found in the literature, we quote here the following, absolutely sincere statements from Müller's compendium *Lebensnerven und Lebenstriebe*, a work of unquestionable seriousness: "Individuals of the various species are protected from extinction until the preservation of that species has been guaranteed" (p. 955, third edition), an approximate paraphrase of which would be the categorical imperative "Reproduce yourself and die, human fly!" And again:

> To ensure that single individuals not shirk the task of reproduction, compliance with the drive to detumefy affords relief and a diminution of tension; the fulfillment of the instinct to concretize has been invested by nature with the most intensely voluptuous feelings. . . . By whatever name one may call the Creator of all living creatures, the world spirit which has devised the laws for their preservation and propagation, our language will never do justice to His nature, since no human brain is capable of comprehending it [p. 973].

Expressions of this kind of agnostic arrogance have, it seems to me, no place in matters of science. On the contrary, we want to and can learn what nature in us, or if one prefers, God in us, really is and how it works.

In areas where scientific knowledge is lacking for want of appropriate investigative methods, researchers usually become elegiac, for which, in view of the all-encompassing nature of the sexual laws, they can hardly be blamed. A critique of the mixture of mechanistic-materialistic and religious thinking prevailing at present will be justified only when it can also offer proof of the earthly nature of the mystical experience.

In short, there are as many interpretations of the sexual process—not counting the ethical—as there are specialized fields of sexology. The science that has gained relatively the deepest insight, psychoanalysis, also developed a special drive metaphysics in those areas where it stepped outside scientific psychology. True, psychoanalysis had revealed the psychic mechanisms of the libido, but it was unable to establish any fundamental principle of sexuality.

Some people may consider it presumptuous to criticize the compartmentalization of sexology, since sexuality is so basic that it would be virtually impossible to devise an all-encompassing formulation. Because this is the very objection I myself had made, I had to state very exactly how it was gradually refuted. To this end it was necessary to describe the quarrel between the mechanistic and the vitalistic views in biology, not, to be sure, to settle the dispute but rather to bring out those issues which had previously stood in the way of a solution to the problem of sexuality.*

It is no accident that the orgasm, although it is the core

* See *The Function of the Orgasm* [New York: Farrar, Straus and Giroux, 1973], Chapter IX.—Ed.

issue of sexuality, has heretofore been given little commensurate notice and clarification. The investigation of the orgasm combines all the methodological difficulties encountered individually in other sexual fields. The problem of the orgasm brings together all the various directions and specialized spheres of sexual investigation. It is not only a psychic experience with certain psychic prerequisites and hence a matter for psychoanalysis, it is also a physical experience characterized by tension-relaxation in its purest form and is hence a matter for physiology as well. According to present research, it is a basic phenomenon of life, at least among creatures that copulate and those that produce and discharge sexual substance. Whether the orgasm also governs sexuality in all sexually differentiated creatures, whether perhaps it even constitutes a basic phenomenon in all living things, is the very question the present exploration in sex economy attempts to clarify. The psychoanalytic problem of the orgasm provided the starting point from which sex economy evolved. If it was not to become yet another specialized view of sexuality, if it claimed to deal with the fundamental laws of sexuality, to be, that is to say, *the* sexology, it first had to blaze its own investigative trail, to define how these fundamental laws might be arrived at, when each sexual specialization had its own methods and concepts. Furthermore, it had to avoid the danger inherent in the assumption that it was a specialized science, because if sexuality is the life problem itself, then sex economy would be the theory of life itself. No such presumption is intended. All the same, we will not give up all claim to the discovery of basic sexual laws.

1944   Wilhelm Reich

CHAPTER ONE

Orgastic Potency

Orgastic potency is to be understood as the ability to achieve full resolution of existing sexual need-tension, an ability that is seldom impaired in healthy individuals. It is lacking in neurotics.

Is it possible to define a standard of orgastic potency despite the diversity of individual sexual needs? An objection has been raised that I am describing an ideal that is not even approximately attainable in reality. I disagree. I am in fact referring to a very real state of affairs. People who are sexually unimpaired (under the circumstances of current sexual upbringing they are found only rarely) describe their experience at the height of excitation, and their satisfaction, in such unequivocal terms that it becomes easy to establish criteria for orgastic potency. Where these criteria are lacking or are inadequately fulfilled, insufficient satisfaction can be recognized regardless of the usually misleading statements of the patients themselves. In diagnosing the degree and quality of a disturbance in orgastic potency it is not enough to ask "Does intercourse satisfy you?" All the typical indicators must be discussed. Many women, for instance, who have never had an orgasm claim to be satisfied, although they experience only partial excitation.

Whereas with women the line between orgastic capability and incapability is very sharply drawn, with men the matter is more complicated, because orgastic excitation is tied to seminal discharge; thus no sharp division can be made. Many men know that they remain unsatisfied. In other men satisfaction is sufficiently great as to obscure a lack of complete gratification. But even in these individuals there is a deficit, however small, that reveals itself as a feeling of disgust or leaden weariness after coition. Plainly, the necessary measure of satisfaction has not been attained.

In evaluating the situation, more depends on the actual fulfillment of needs than on the subjective feeling of "satisfaction." Proof of this is to be found clinically in patients who at the start of treatment claim to feel satisfaction in coitus only to recognize their disturbance retroactively when, in the course of treatment, their capacity for gratification increases. From the economic point of view, a clear distinction must be made between sexual activity and sexual satisfaction. Although those who have an overly active "sexual life" may well appear to be particularly potent, one of the causes of their hypersexuality is actually their limited capacity for satisfaction. The prerequisite for correct assessment is an exact inquiry into the details of coitus.

In women, note should be taken of whether the orgasm is clitoral or vaginal; the difference is qualitative as well as quantitative. Although a clitoral orgasm can relieve gross tensions, it usually occurs under such complex psychic conditions (as, for instance, real situation female, fantasy male) that it cannot replace the economic function of vaginal orgasm. Proof of this is the clearly evident sexual stasis in women who experience only clitoral orgasms.

The degree of genital satisfaction may oscillate between

partial and total. The consequence of experiencing only partial orgastic satisfaction over a prolonged period, as, for instance, in a marriage of long standing, will be sexual stasis.

The postulation of a characteristic type of orgastic potency is also supported clinically. Thus, following elimination of a potency disturbance, the curve representing experience of orgastic pleasure automatically assumes the form of the orgastic potency curve.[1]

The following is a report of a patient's progress during treatment for premature ejaculation, excessive masturbation, and other symptoms. From age eight he had masturbated one to three times a day without guilt or conscious fear of harming himself. Usually at suppertime, or when he went to bed, he would begin to think about *having* to masturbate, even though he was not the least bit excited. Once in bed, he would start to read with the intention of masturbating in half an hour's time. When he began to masturbate, his penis was flaccid, eventually becoming erect through physical stimulation. All the while he would be contemplating to whom he should "dedicate" his masturbation that day; it was "like a Mass I had to read for someone." Fantasizing deliberately, he would gradually become aroused. His thoughts would then wander to trivialities—about business, banal events of the day, and so forth. When his mind wandered, excitation waned, only to increase at the renewed onset of fantasy. This occurred several times and on the average lasted half an hour. Finally he achieved a climax. The physical spasms were strong, and the ensuing satisfaction restored him to the unexcited state that existed just prior to masturbation. At my request he drew a curve to illustrate the course of his excitation.

[1] In the interest of clarity we shall portray orgasm disturbances as curves.

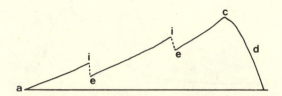

FIGURE 1.　*Course of excitation during masturbation*

  a. no excitation
  i. involuntary interruption of fantasy activity
  e. excitation with voluntary resumption of fantasy
  c. climax
  d. decrease of excitation

Even before falling ill with the neurosis (erythro-phobia), he had suffered from premature ejaculation, which had grown worse in the interim. (He had been only relatively potent with a married woman who fulfilled certain sexual conditions.) Intercourse usually lasted approximately half a minute, and foreplay was greatly prolonged. Coitus ended in greater satisfaction than masturbation, especially when his climax was achieved simultaneously with the woman's. Afterward, he was left with a sense of well-being, the opposite of his feeling after masturbation. Following intercourse with other women, where ejaculation occurred shortly after penetration, he experienced only disgust and aversion. The curve in Figure 2 represents the course of the orgasm with the woman he loved. Figure 3 depicts excitation with subsequent premature ejaculation.

When he began treatment, sexual practice consisted of placing his fully erect penis between the woman's thighs (at the same time entertaining conscious homosexual fantasies). The reason he gave for using this method was that he did not want to cause pregnancy. However, in his

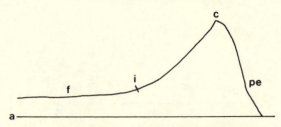

FIGURE 2. *Sexual intercourse with facultative potency (duration from intromission about half a minute)*

    a.   no excitation
    f.   prolonged foreplay
    i.   intromission
    c.   climax
  pe.   a remainder of psychic excitation

dreams the fear of entering the vagina was so pronounced that I was able to make it clear to him that all his reasons were mere rationalizations. At first he had wanted to prove me wrong. But during the next attempt at inter-

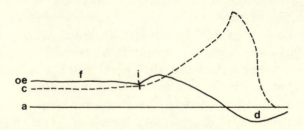

FIGURE 3. *Sexual excitation with subsequent ejaculatio praecox*

  a.   no excitation
 oe.   overexcitation
  f.   prolonged foreplay
  i.   intromission and shallow climax
  d.   subsequent intense disgust
  c.   line of comparison

course "it exploded" before he had even assumed the coital position. Analysis of dreams following this fiasco indicated that he feared a dangerous "thing" that he believed to exist inside the vagina. Later he himself interpreted the prematurity of the ejaculation as an expression of his fear of "tarrying too long in the lion's den."

Once this fear and other significant elements were brought to consciousness, intercourse became successful. According to his own report, he had never experienced such satisfaction. He spent considerably less time in foreplay as his fear of intercourse subsided. With the woman he loved, intercourse itself, as he reported, now lasted approximately three times as long as it had prior to the neurotic illness (approximately one and a half to two minutes). Excitation began slowly and then increased rapidly. For the first time, he had no fantasies during intercourse and felt pleasantly tired in his entire body afterwards, without experiencing the "heaviness in my head," as was the case following masturbation or intercourse with premature ejaculation. This course of excitation is portrayed by the curve in Figure 4.

Several months after the conclusion of treatment, the patient informed me that he felt, among other things, completely potent and satisfied. Intercourse now lasted approximately five minutes, he had no fantasies, and he did not feel "empty" afterward.

A comparison of the figures shows that the incline of the second curve is shorter than that of the fourth. The great trust the patient put in the woman he loved, as well as certain conditions favorable for sexual contact, rendered erective potency and considerable satisfaction possible, although fear of intercourse caused prolongation of foreplay and considerable curtailment of friction. However, the duration of friction was almost tripled when

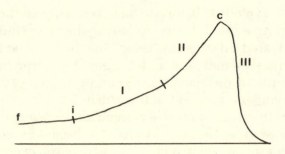

FIGURE 4. *Course of excitation following analysis of fear (duration approximately two minutes)*

 f. foreplay (shorter)
 i. intromission
 I. slow increase of excitation
 II. rapid rise to climax
 c. climax
 III. steep decline of excitation with gentle evanescence

fear of coitus became conscious. In premature ejaculation, friction was almost nonexistent, the orgasm was shallow and prolonged, and the meager sensation of pleasure was accompanied by intense disgust, in contrast to coitus that was free of anxiety.

In coitus without fear, disgust, or fantasies, *the intensity of end pleasure in the orgasm is therefore directly dependent on the degree of sexual tension focused on the genitals:* the steeper the "incline" of excitation, the more intense the end pleasure.

The following description of the satisfying sexual act refers only to the course of several typical biologically determined phases and behavioral patterns. I have not taken foreplay activities into account because they are determined by individual needs and exhibit no regular patterns.

The Phase of Voluntary Control of Excitation

1. Erection is pleasurable, not painful, as would be the case if the genitals were overexcited. The female genitals become hyperemic and slippery due to profuse secretion of the genital glands.* The clitoris is initially excited upon penetration of the penis, but in orgastically potent women the excitation is immediately transferred to the vagina without clitoral competition. An important indication of orgastic potency in men is the urge to penetrate. Erection can occur without this urge, as is revealed in some erectively potent narcissistic characters, and in cases of satyriasis.

2. The male partner is tender. Pathological deviations from this attitude may be seen in aggression stemming from sadistic impulses, as in some erectively potent compulsion neurotics, and in the inactivity of the passive-feminine character. Tenderness is also lacking in "masturbational coitus" with an unloved object. Normally the activity of the woman does not differ in any way from that of the man. The passivity that is usual nowadays is pathological, frequently the result of masochistic rape fantasies.

3. With the penetration of the penis the level of pleasure, which has remained approximately the same during foreplay, suddenly increases equally in both man and woman. The feeling on the part of the man of being "pulled in" corresponds to the woman's feeling of "sucking in" the penis.

---

* Recent investigations have established that the "genital glands" (Bartholin's glands) contribute only minimally to vaginal lubrication. The latter is a "transudate-like reaction" or "sweating" which makes its appearance early in the sexual response cycle due to the marked congestion of the venous plexus surrounding the walls of the vagina.—Ed.

FIGURE 5. *Typical phases of the sexual act in which
both male and female are orgastically potent
(duration approximately 5-20 minutes)*

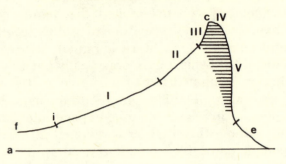

  a. no excitation
  f. foreplay
  i. intromission
   I. phase of voluntary control of excitation increase
     and prolongation which is not yet harmful
  II. (6a-d) phase of involuntary muscle contractions
     and automatic increase of excitation
 III. (7) sudden sharp incline to the climax (*c*)
 IV. (8) orgasm
  V. (9-10) steep drop of the excitation
  e. exhaustion

4. The man's urge to penetrate deep into the woman
increases but does not assume the form of a sadistic "desire
to bore through her," as it does in compulsion neurotics.
Through mutual, spontaneous, and effortless friction, the
excitation becomes concentrated on the surface and glans
of the penis and on the posterior parts of the mucous mem-
brane of the vagina. The sensation that characteristically
heralds and then accompanies the discharge of semen is
completely absent, in contrast to cases of premature
ejaculation. The body is still less excited than the genitals.
Awareness is entirely centered on the pleasure sensations;

the ego participates actively, inasmuch as it tries to exhaust all possibilities for pleasure and to achieve the highest degree of tension before the onset of the orgasm. Conscious intentions obviously play no part in this process. It occurs automatically on the basis of previous individual experience and through change of position, type of friction, rhythm, and so on. Potent men and women report that the slower and more gentle the frictions and the more closely synchronized, the stronger the pleasure sensations. (Such movement presupposes a highly developed ability to identify with one's partner.) Pathological counterparts may be seen in the urge for violent friction, as in sadistic-compulsive character types who suffer from penis anesthesia and the inability to ejaculate, as well as in the nervous haste of individuals suffering from premature ejaculation. With the exception of tender utterances, orgastically potent men and women never laugh or talk during the sexual act. Both talking and laughing indicate severe disturbances in the ability to surrender oneself, which demands undivided absorption in the pleasure sensations. Men who regard surrender as "feminine" are usually orgastically disturbed.

5. In this phase, interruption of the friction is in itself pleasurable because of the special sensations that attend this pause and do not require psychic exertion. The level of excitation sinks slightly, without subsiding altogether as in pathological cases, thus prolonging the act. Even withdrawal of the penis is not unpleasurable if it occurs after a restful interval. When friction is resumed, the excitation increases steadily beyond the level reached prior to the interruption. It gradually encompasses the entire body, while the genitals maintain a more or less constant level of excitation. Finally, a new and usually sudden increase of genital excitation results in the second phase.

The Phase of Involuntary
Muscle Contraction

6. In this phase it is no longer possible to exert voluntary control over the course of excitation, which exhibits the following characteristics:

a. The increase of excitation controls the entire personality, causing an acceleration of pulse and deep exhalation.

b. The physical excitation once again focuses on the genitals without thereby reducing the excitation throughout the body. A sensation sets in which can best be described as an overflowing of excitation to the genitals.

c. This excitation first causes waves of reflex contractions of the entire musculature of the genitals and pelvic floor, the wave crests coinciding with the complete penetration of the penis and the troughs coinciding with penile retraction. As soon as retraction exceeds a certain limit, spasmodic contractions that accelerate ejaculation occur. In the woman the smooth musculature of the vagina now also contracts.

d. In this stage, interruption of the act is absolutely unpleasurable for both partners. The muscle contractions that lead to the orgasm in the woman and to ejaculation in the man will be spasmodic instead of rhythmic, causing great discomfort and occasionally even pain in the pelvic floor and the small of the back. In addition, because of the spasms, ejaculation will occur earlier than it would had the rhythm been maintained.

Voluntary protraction of the first phase of the sexual act (stages one through five) is harmless up to a certain degree, and has the effect of increasing pleasure. In the second phase, however, interruption or any other attempt to modify the course of excitation is harmful, irritating the nervous system itself. This will be discussed later in the clinical sections involving such conditions as neurasthenia, the effects of coitus interruptus, and so forth.

7. Through increases in the strength and frequency of the involuntary muscle contractions, excitation rises steeply and rapidly to the climax (III to *c* in Figure 5); normally this coincides with the first ejaculatory muscle contractions in the man.

8. Now a more or less extreme *blurring of consciousness* takes place. The frictions increase spontaneously after having ceased briefly at the "peak" of the climax, and the urge to penetrate "completely" becomes more intense with each ejaculatory muscle contraction. In the woman the muscle contractions follow the same pattern as in the man. The psychic difference is to be found in the healthy woman's desire to "receive completely" during and just after the climax. (The reciprocal identifications and further behavioral differences in the two sexes will be discussed in a different context.)

9. Orgastic excitation takes hold of the body, inducing strong convulsions of the entire musculature. Self-observation by healthy individuals of both sexes, as well as analysis of certain orgasm disturbances, indicates that what we term release of tension and perceive as motor discharge (descending curve of the orgasm) is predominantly a result of excitation flowing back from the genitals to the body. This reflux is experienced as a sudden decrease in tension.

Thus the climax constitutes the turning point, at which

the flow of excitation toward the genitals reverses direction. Only complete reversal of direction secures satisfaction, which has a twofold implication: excitation reversion and genital unburdening.

10. Before the zero point is reached, excitation fades in a gentle curve and is immediately replaced by a pleasant physical and psychic limpness. Usually there is also a strong need for sleep. Sensual interaction is now extinguished, but a "satisfied" tender relationship to the partner persists, augmented by a feeling of gratitude.

In contrast, the orgastically impotent experience leaden fatigue, disgust, aversion, indifference, and occasionally even hate toward the partner. (In satyriasis and nymphomania, sexual excitation does not diminish.) The woman frequently experiences insomnia, a significant indication of lack of satisfaction. On the other hand, one cannot simply jump to the conclusion that because patients report that they fall asleep immediately after intercourse, they are therefore sexually satisfied.

Reviewing the two phases of the sexual act, it will be seen that the first is characterized predominantly by sensory experience and the second by motor experience. The suddenly heightened transition into the second phase and the total dissipation of excitation are the most important hallmarks of orgastic potency. In Figure 5 the shaded portion of the curve indicates the involuntary vegetative release. There are partial dissolutions of excitation that are orgasm*like*; hitherto these were regarded as the actual release. But clinical experience shows that, as a result of general sexual repression, people have lost the capacity for complete involuntary vegetative surrender. *By orgastic potency I mean just this ultimate, heretofore unrecognized element of excitability and release of tension.* It is this that constitutes the primal biological function that man has in common with all living creatures. All feelings for nature derive from this function or from a yearning for it.

It is commonly held that the delay of the female orgasm is physiological; attempts were even made to explain this fact biologically. For example, the delayed onset of the female orgasm was interpreted to have the "biological purpose" of inducing a second orgasm in the male to ensure fertilization. It is true that women frequently experience greater difficulty than men in achieving orgasm. Any consideration of this fact, however, must disregard those cases in which a (relative) delay of the woman's orgasm is caused by the premature climax of the man. Fürbringer, in accordance with Lowenfeld's ten-minute standard, is of the opinion that normal coitus lasts from five to fifteen minutes. This corresponds to my own estimates. It cannot yet be termed pathological if a man ejaculates after one to three minutes, but we shall also not characterize him as potent, because we know that such ". . . premature ejaculations which are natural for certain altogether healthy men . . ." (Fürbringer) are likewise based on inhibitions. I call to mind the patient who, prior to analysis, achieved a relatively satisfying orgasm in half a minute and then more than doubled the duration of friction after becoming conscious of his fear of coitus.

Apart from this issue, there are other reasons for delayed orgasms in otherwise healthy women. The double sexual standard obligates women to reject sexuality to a far greater extent than it does men, and the desire to be a man, which need not prevent satisfaction completely, may well have a disturbing effect on the course of excitation. If these inhibitors are absent, the course of female excitation does not differ from that of the male.

The orgasm of both sexes is more intense when the climaxes of genital excitation coincide. This occurs very frequently in individuals who are able to focus both sensuality and tenderness on one partner and meet with a corresponding response. And it is often the rule when the love relationship is neither internally nor externally disturbed. In such cases at least conscious fantasy activity is totally eliminated; the ego is concentrated exclusively on pleasure sensations. *A further characteristic of orgastic potency is the ability to focus temporarily the entire affective personality on the genital experience despite any conflicts.*

Whether unconscious fantasy activity also ceases cannot be immediately ascertained, although certain indications suggest that it does. Fantasies that are not allowed to become conscious can only be disturbing. Among the fantasies that may accompany coitus, we must differentiate between those attuned to the sexual experience and those at variance with it. If all sexual interest is at least momentarily focused on the sexual partner, unconscious fantasy will become superfluous. (It would run contrary to real experience, since one fantasizes only what is unattainable in reality.) There is a *genuine* transference from the original object to the partner because there is a basic correspondence of the two that enables the latter to replace the object of the fantasy. However, if transference of sexual interests results merely from neurotic striving for the original object, despite the fact that the partner does not correspond basically with the fantasy object and the inner capacity for genuine transference is lacking, no illusion will eliminate the vague feeling of fraudulence in the relationship. With genuine transference, there is no disappointment following intercourse. Without it, disappointment is unavoidable. We may assume that in the latter instance fantasy activity does not cease during intercourse but actually serves to maintain the illusion, whereas in the former the original object loses its appeal and hence its power to generate fantasies; it is re-created in the partner. In genuine transference there is no overvaluation of the sexual partner; characteristics contrary to those of the original object are recognized and tolerated. In false transference, idealization is excessive and illusion predominates; negative characteristics are not perceived, and fantasy activity must not cease lest the illusion be lost.

The more fantasy must be strained to reconcile the partner to the ideal, the weaker sexual pleasure will be in intensity and sex-economic value. Whether the intensity of sexual experience is reduced, and if so, to what degree, depends entirely upon the disharmony that accompanies every interpersonal relationship of some duration. The greater the fixation on the original object and the incapacity for genuine transference, the greater the expenditure of energy required to overcome the rejection of the real partner, and the sooner the reduction of sexual pleasure will lead to pathological disturbance.

CHAPTER TWO

The Neurotic Conflict

Freud discovered that every neurotic and psychotic symptom, regardless of how meaningless it may appear, has, in fact, significant content which can be completely integrated into the total experience of the individual, assuming exact data are available. Neurotic symptoms arise from conflicts between primitive drive demands and moral requirements that prohibit drive satisfaction. The "inner denial" of drive satisfaction in psychiatric patients derives from external restrictions of drives they experienced during their upbringing. The conflict between drive ego and moral ego, therefore, was originally a conflict between drive ego and external reality, and it retains this character in some psychotics and in impulsive psychopaths.[1] However, in the neurotic, as opposed to the psychotic and the psychopath, a substantial portion of the personality has managed to successfully adjust to reality, while another portion has suffered developmental arrest in an early psychic phase, the inevitable result being a conflict between opposing impulses. It is characteristic of

[1] Cf. Aichhorn, "Verwahrloste Jugend," *International Psychoanalytische Bibliothek*, Bd. XIX, 1925; and Reich, "Der triebhafte Charakter," *Neue Arbeiten zur ärztlichen Psychoanalyse*, Nr. IV, 1925 ["The Impulsive Character," in *Early Writings*, Vol. I (New York: Farrar, Straus and Giroux, 1975)].

neurotic personalities that the moral ego has neither the courage to tolerate drive satisfaction nor the strength to condemn or subdue the drive demands in some appropriate manner. This is due to a lack of, or a deficiency in, the initial prerequisite, namely, consciousness of the drive impulses. The ego is startled by the slightest indication of an "immoral" impulse and purges it through "repression." This process can assume various forms, from a simple refusal to acknowledge the impulse, or a disregarding of it through emphasizing the opposite of the tabooed drive, to utter exclusion of the idea from consciousness (hysterical amnesia) and the interdiction of any motor release of the corresponding degree of affect. The impact of the repressed drive demand, however, is by no means weakened. On the contrary, it is intensified by the "stasis" of unreleased drive energy. The danger now lies in the impulse being no longer under the control of conscious thought. Under certain conditions the impulse will break through the "countercathexis," or ego "resistance." But this "breakthrough of repression," which constitutes the second phase of the neurotic process, can be only partial, for the ego defense also relies on powerful psychic controls which may be encompassed by the term "morals," in its popular sense. The result is a disguised drive gratification, which remains unrecognized as such by the conscious mind or, to the extent that it is less disguised, is perceived as alien to the ego—as a compulsion—and is rejected.

Up to this point, there was nothing to object to in Freud's findings. Violent disagreement first arose over his theory that sexual desires are a regular component of repressed drive impulses. To those who accused psychoanalysis of "pansexualism," Freud replied that, first, mankind's antisexual morality is itself a contributing factor in the formation of neuroses, which cannot even come into existence unless the ego contravened its own drives; and second, in addition to sexual desires, selfishness, cruelty, and other impulses also participate in the formation of neuroses (although less frequently and less insistently). This reply availed him nothing. The academic world did not take the trouble to critically examine what it thought could be disposed of with the catchword "pansexualism."

Initially labeled as figments of the imagination, findings of psychoanalysis were assimilated, cautiously, by only a few people, who accepted them in part as their own, new discoveries, and in part in diluted or distorted form. Very few used the specified method to validate the theory.

I have reason for mentioning the attitudes then prevailing among the opponents of psychoanalysis. Wrongly imputing politico-cultural motives to Freud, these men felt instinctively that his sexual-political approach to cultural criticism implied a threat to their own position. Yet from the outset he had stressed that he was not attacking "civilization"; that his adversaries were confusing "sexual" and "genital"; that in his teachings, too, "moral obligations" were given their due. In his later writings, such as *Civilization and Its Discontents*, Freud specifically represented the conflict between sexual happiness and the evolution of civilization as insoluble, though he declared himself a proponent of the latter. His efforts remained unsuccessful; the world of "cultural values" sensed its own downfall. Yet in spite of their bitter struggle, neither Freud nor his opponents guessed where the danger to "civilization" really lay.

Eventually, psychoanalysis completely adapted itself to the world, for the only real danger had lain in the earliest attempts at a psychoanalytic formulation of the relationship between the sexuality-morality conflict and psychic health.

The critical point, which his opponents unconsciously perceived, and which Freud himself never even discussed, lay in what was still an obscure area of clinical investigation. Freud had shown that there are tendencies (pregenital partial drives) that exist parallel to genital sexuality but have nothing to do with the genital zone. Their aim is to achieve satisfaction through stimulation of certain "erogenous zones" (mouth, anus, skin, etc.), and they must be termed sexual, since they play an important role in the "foreplay" of normal sexual intercourse—and when perverted, demand exclusive sexual satisfaction. In his writings, the emphasis Freud placed on the difference between the terms "genital" and "sexual" sounded at times like an effort to offer reassurance about the implications of his discoveries. However, he was unsuccessful in this; emotional opposition to his theories of infantile sexuality and anal eroticism continued unabated.

Based on this broadening of the concept of sexuality, Freud concluded that no neurosis could occur without *sexual* conflict, that is, that pregenital partial drives, too, emerge as symptoms. By this he meant that individual neurotic symptoms result directly from, and provide camouflaged satisfaction for, some repressed partial drive. Thus, for example, repressed anality is active in nervous constipation; oral eroticism, in hysterical vomiting; genitality, in *arc-de-cercle;* sadism, in certain compulsive acts and compulsion-neurotic methods of avoidance. An actual conflict may produce neurosis in any area, assuming there is a corresponding predisposition.

In the psychoanalytic description of the neurotic process, psychic conflict and partial drive were seen as the motive force and the content of the symptom. Genital impotence and frigidity were viewed as neurotic symptoms among the other neurotic symptoms. According to opinion then prevailing, partial drives, although related to each other, were held to be independent drive aims—biologically given units within the totality of the sexual drive. Any specific dependence of neurosis on genital disturbances was unknown, as was cure by their removal. *Where the continuing nourishment of the neurosis actually came from was a question that went unasked.* The contention that there are neuroses without genital disturbance, which for the most part was upheld until 1923, effectively barred the way to an understanding of the general condition of blocked energy discharge. Neurotic symptoms were considered to be circumscribed disturbances in an otherwise sound personality. The connection between symptom and character was not grasped. From the time Alfred Adler had attempted to replace the theory of sexuality with his doctrine of the nervous character, there had been a strong revulsion against any preoccupation with the problem of character. Only individual character traits, like symptoms, were traced back to their instinctual foundations.

This summary will explain why the following proposition encountered strong resistance when I introduced it to the Psychoanalytic Clinic. I maintained that *disturbance of the genital function always plays the principal dynamic role in establishing the neurotic-reaction basis upon which the neurotic conflict is then built. Because of its relation to the neurotic process, its removal is crucial to the treatment of the neurosis.*

The primary proof of the validity of this view is the fact

that *there is no neurosis or psychosis without disturbances of the genital function.* In almost all cases these disturbances are not subtle. They literally involve elementary functions of sexual intercourse and sexual attitudes in general. Most frequently one encounters sexual timidity and neurotic abstinence, in addition to all forms of erective impotence known in sexological literature (total, partial, and facultative), disturbances in ejaculation (ejaculatio praecox ante portas and impotentia ejaculandi), and frigidity (total sexual frigidity, vaginal anesthesia and hypesthesia, vaginismus, etc.). The severity of the potency disturbance corresponds to the severity of the neurosis; the same holds true for character neuroses manifesting no symptoms at all. Among those suffering acutely from the symptoms of the climacteric, typical findings yield not a single patient who is able to report satisfying sexual activity during the period prior to the climacteric. In concluding this summary, the cases of addiction and other forms of impulsive behavior, which always manifest grossly disturbed genitality, should also be mentioned.

The first statistical study was comprised of 338 individuals who sought treatment at the Vienna Psychoanalytic Out-patient Clinic between November 1923 and November 1924.

DATA GATHERED FROM ROUTINE ANAMNESIS

166 male patients		*91 female patients*	
supposedly potent	17	without vaginal anesthesia or hypesthesia	0
supposedly completely impotent	18	supposedly only frigid	6
neurotic and abstinent	69	neurotic and abstinent	27
neurotic with erective impotence	27	neurotic and frigid	37

166 male patients		*91 female patients*	
neurotic with ejaculatio praecox	14	neurotic due to actual marital conflicts and frigid	12
perversion with erective impotence	9	climacteric	9
climacteric	5		
actual-neurotic illness due to coitus interruptus	7		

For the remaining thirty-six men and forty-five women, there were no anamnestic findings on genital functioning. For the most part these people could not be questioned on such matters because of their great timidity during the first consultation. Among the male patients, there were only seventeen who reported that they were potent. The majority of such patients, when they come for treatment, turn out to be suffering from a greater or lesser degree of erective impotence. Those who are actually erectively potent are to be found among erythrophobics, compulsive characters, and phallic-narcissistic characters.

The second study consisted of cases I treated myself.

41 male patients

hysterical and abstinent with erective potency	4
compulsion-neurotic, abstinent due to ascetic ideology	6
hysterical with severely reduced erective potency	1
compulsion-neurotic with erective impotence	1
hysterical with ejaculatio praecox	2
hypochondriacal-neurasthenic with genital asthenia (ejaculatio praecox ante portas without erection)	4
erythrophobic and abstinent due to fear of impotence	3
morally insane (swindlers and addicts) with ejaculatio praecox	2
kleptomaniac with erective impotence	1

41 male patients (cont.)

neurasthenic with ejaculative impotence	1
impotent only, neurotic character	4
postencephalitic with erective impotence following influenza	1
homosexual and deviant with erective impotence with women	3
impulsive character with erective impotence	1
healthy, no potency disturbance	1
erectively potent, narcissistic homosexual, lack of satisfaction in intercourse	1
erectively potent, compulsive character, lack of satisfaction in intercourse	4
erectively potent with satyriasis, lack of satisfaction in intercourse	1

31 female patients

hysterical and abstinent due to fear of sex	7
compulsion-neurotic, rejecting of sex, and abstinent	4
hysterical with vaginal anesthesia	9
compulsion-neurotic and frigid	3
cycloid with chronic hypochondriacal neurasthenia, sexual timidity	1
impulsive character, frigid or vaginally anesthetic	3
nymphomaniacal with masochistic perversion and vaginal anesthesia during intercourse	1
advanced epileptic, frigid	1
hysteroepileptic, with vaginal anesthesia	1
paranoiac, frigid	1
no disturbances of genital functions	0

These findings speak for themselves. Since 1925 clinical experience—including the many hundreds of cases I personally evaluated in the course of two years at my Sexual Guidance Center for Working People and Office Employees in Vienna and, after 1930, at centers in Germany—has demonstrated that there is no neurosis without

a disturbance of the genital function. The fact is confirmed, but it requires very detailed proof.

From a sex-economic point of view (and what other
perspective on impotence could have practical value?) it is
inconsequential whether a woman has more or less sexual
feeling, or whether or not a man is erectively potent.
What is important is whether the orgasm is disturbed.

CHAPTER THREE

Disturbances of the Orgasm

Disturbances of erective and ejaculative potency must be distinguished from disturbances of "end pleasure" (Freud) or "detumescence" (Moll). In women the less easily differentiated disturbances of sexual functioning are combined under the heading of frigidity, vaginal anesthesia, and hypesthesia. However, one also finds isolated disturbances of the orgasm function in women who experience normal precoital excitation. Valuable contributions toward understanding orgastic disturbances in women, and their significance in the emergence of organic illnesses, have been made by Kehrer[1] from the gynecological standpoint. Stekel's *Frigidity in Woman in Relation to Her Love Life* and *Impotence in the Male* offer copious and worthwhile material, but are not adequately interpreted. This also applies to the otherwise extremely valuable contributions in sexological literature.[2] Perhaps

[1] *Ursachen und Behandlung der Unfruchtbarkeit* (Leipzig, 1922).

[2] To obviate any possible accusations that the literature on the orgasm was ignored, I should like to state clearly that, to the best of my knowledge, no comprehensive clinical treatise on this subject exists. In Marcuse's worthy and other-

43

the fact that psychoanalytic literature makes no contributions to our topic can be attributed to certain qualms attached to using the analytic interview to discuss the culmination of human sexual experience in detail (and only the details yield important insights). Patients find it hard to discuss such matters of their own accord. Furthermore, very few patients are able to offer information; indeed, they do not even understand the questions being asked of them. Even after I had begun to devote serious attention to impotence and frigidity as crucial symptoms that appear in every neurosis, the manifold disturbances of the orgasm itself escaped me.

In the course of my investigations, the exposing and analytic clarification of the orgasm problem, which has proven fruitful in totally unexpected ways for understanding the sex-economic problem of the neurosis, made it necessary to attribute sex-economic significance to the concept of potency.[3] In so doing I relied on the theory first formulated and proved by Freud, namely, that people become neurotic because of deficient gratification, and that libido stasis constitutes the core of neurosis. I have furnished proof that sexual repression disturbs endpleasure wherever it has not already obstructed the search for a partner (abstinence) or interfered in the forepleasure

---

wise accurately compiled *Handbuch der Sexualwissenschaft*, the terms "acme" and "orgasm" are not treated specifically. The scattered remarks in the sections on coitus and impotence also indicate how limited the interest in the function of the orgasm is in scientific circles. In less recent sexological literature, i.e., the works of Bloch, Havelock Ellis, Moll, Krafft-Ebing, Forel, etc., I found no basically significant information on this topic. The monographs by Urbach (*Zeitschrift für Sexualwissenschaft*, Bd. VIII, 1921) and Vaerting (*Zeitschrift für Sexualwissenschaft*, Bd. II, 1915) treat the orgasm problem from a strictly eugenic standpoint, in keeping with the general tendency to neglect psychological considerations of sexual life in favor of eugenics and physiology.

[3] "Die therapeutische Bedeutung der Genitallibido," *Internationale Zeitschrift für Psychoanalyse*, XI, 1925 ["The Therapeutic Significance of Genital Libido," in *Early Writings*, Vol. I (New York: Farrar, Straus and Giroux, 1975)].

mechanisms (erective impotence, anesthesia), thereby upsetting the equilibrium of libidinal excitation and causing disorder in the sexual economy.

All psychic disturbances of end pleasure may be understood as deviations from the criteria of orgastic potency as I have described it. By "orgastic impotence" I mean the inability—even under the most favorable external circumstances—to achieve satisfaction that corresponds to existing sexual tension and to sexual needs. Since orgastically impotent individuals usually have a limited capacity for work, permanent energy stasis results. In this respect the orgastically impotent are even worse off than those who live in abstinence or those who lack genital excitability, because they live in a state of significantly heightened tension caused by genital stimuli, and are unable to achieve the balance that is, by this very condition, made all the more necessary.

One can differentiate four basic disturbances of orgastic potency, assuming the precoital functions are intact:

1. *reduced orgastic potency:* for inner reasons the orgasm does not fulfill sexual requirements (masturbation, masturbational coition);
2. *dispersion of the orgasm:* excitation is directly disturbed during intercourse (acute neurasthenia);
3. *complete inability to achieve an orgasm* (vaginal anesthesia, hypesthesia, genital asthenia, frigidity);
4. *nymphomanic sexual excitation* (nymphomania, satyriasis).

Reduced Orgastic Potency

Chronically reduced end satisfaction is seen primarily in individuals who, for inner reasons, cannot find the right partner: in habitual masturbators, sexual cynics, covert homosexuals, perpetual bachelors, and schizoid-introverted individuals with deficient object relations; in men manifesting a permanent split of the genital impulse into its tender and sensual components; and in men who continually have intercourse with prostitutes who do not specifically correspond to the original object. Only the reduction of orgastic potency that, in time, occurs in masturbators is of clinical interest.

In masturbation the strain to hold on to the fantasy, to vary it, and to reproduce the pleasure sensations experienced during intercourse reduces satisfaction to such a degree that the release of existing tension is very incomplete. In this regard intercourse with unloved partners is in every respect similar to masturbation; the psychic aims always remain unsatisfied. The effort needed for fantasy-building and the unfulfilled longing for love lower the degree of physical satisfaction as well. We cannot agree with Stekel that masturbation is an adequate means of satisfaction for some people. Clinical experience leaves no doubt that individuals who do not transcend the physiological stage of pubertal masturbation have remained fixated on childhood objects and are afraid of coitus. Both the fixation on childish patterns and the fear of intercourse are conditioned by the present social order and upbringing, which imbue people with sexual anxiety.

Once the inclination toward masturbation has become established in this manner, it results in increasingly severe and encompassing regression to infantile desires and objects which, in turn, requires intensification of defense measures. This is why so many neuroses erupt shortly after puberty and develop into the struggle against masturbation. If masturbation is completely suppressed, causing somatic stasis to become pathogenic, the physical symptoms in the neurosis become more prominent. Profuse daydreaming, irritability, ill humor, restlessness, difficulty in working, nocturnal emissions, insomnia, and so forth, are usually the first signs of a definite illness. In some cases, elimination by suggestion of guilt feelings and of the fear of having injured oneself will ameliorate the symptoms that have resulted directly from masturbation guilt and the increase in sexual stasis. However, the psychic need for love is not assailable through suggestion; and when the rapport derived from suggestion ceases, this need causes a renewal of guilt feelings, and a tendency toward total abstinence, thus augmenting the physical stasis.

To any unbiased observer these facts are abundantly obvious and need no further detailed clinical verification. However, we should like to cite some examples of how relative orgastic impotence manifests itself in erectively potent neurotics.

A thirty-two-year-old man sought treatment because of spells of timidity and fear of blushing. The illness had begun with his second marriage. He was still attached to his deceased wife and had remarried for economic reasons only. He was erectively potent and in the first consultation reported that he was sexually satisfied. However, I discovered in the early sessions that he had intercourse with his unloved wife approximately once every six weeks, and then only "out of a sense of duty." During coitus he thought of his first wife and measured his second wife against her. After intercourse, which was not even physically satisfying, he was glad that it was "over with."

This case may be viewed as a prototype for a large group of erythrophobics who unconsciously struggle with homosexual fantasies, compensate very well for their impotence with erective potency in heterosexual intercourse, but remain essentially unsatisfied. Such patients have no less sexual stasis than those who force themselves to abstain. Hence it follows that *the contractions of the genital musculature during ejaculation provide satisfaction only when the mechanism of psychic excitation is able to process the pleasure sensations without conflict.* Furthermore, psychic inhibition prevents complete concentration of excitation in the genitals, as well as its release.

The same form of orgastic impotence can be found in erectively potent male compulsion neurotics, though with a different psychic background.

A thirty-five-year-old man with a typical compulsive character and suffering from erective impotence was, after marriage, able to have an erection, thanks to his wife's adeptness. However, his fear of impotence remained, and he was constantly initiating intercourse to prove his potency to himself, making a few thrusts after penetration—"for the sake of practice"—and then discontinuing the act. What physical or psychic excitation he experienced was slight and did not increase, even during ejaculation.

A nineteen-year-old male sought treatment because of compulsive brooding. He had numerous affairs and practiced coitus interruptus. Rarely would he have intercourse with the same girl more than once, because, after intercourse, he despised her even more than before. Coitus was simply an "emptying," similar to defecation. He was also greatly absorbed with having "made it" with a number of girls. Satisfaction was of little importance to him, but he was pleased if the girl's feelings were hurt because he had "dropped her." Later we shall explore in depth the substitution of anal, sadistic, and narcissistic tendencies for genital impulses, as demonstrated so clearly in this case.

A twenty-one-year-old male patient, whose character expressed itself in a distressing compulsion to count, had intercourse very frequently with good erective potency but counted continuously during coitus; his ejaculation was always difficult, taking a long time to occur and lacking any heightened pleasure sensations. Afterward he was depressed, felt disgust and aversion toward the woman, and was unable to fall asleep.

Another form of orgasm disturbance occurs in intercourse that is either too long or too short. If the act does not last long enough, too little sexual excitation from the body is focused in the genitals; ejaculation occurs upon very slight stimulation, as in loveless coitus or premature ejaculation. Very little excitation becomes available for discharge in such instance and, consequently, there is little, if any, gratification. If, on the other hand, forepleasure is prolonged and the orgasm delayed, excitation, rather than being centered in the genitals and discharged orgastically all at once, dissipates itself shallowly; ejaculation occurs with little pleasure.

Dispersion of the Orgasm

Dispersion of the orgasm results from inhibitions which occur during intercourse and not only reduce excitation and cause shallow satisfaction but also disturb the physiological-stimulation sequence itself. Figure 6 illustrates the interruption of the buildup of excitation and the faltering of end pleasure.

Dispersion of the orgasm is seen predominantly in patients complaining of acute manifestations of neurasthenia, that is, irritability, lack of work incentive, fatigue, and vague physical symptoms such as backaches, drawing pains in the legs, and so forth. This allows us to approach

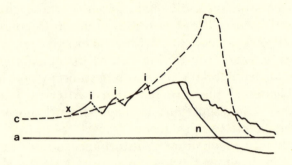

FIGURE 6.   *Curve of the contradiction-filled*
"masturbational coitus"

     a. no excitation
     c. line of comparison
     i. inhibition
     n. nonpleasure
     x. intromission

various questions raised at the time that Freud presented his explanation of the etiology of neurasthenia: "Neurasthenia," he said, "can always be traced to a state of the nervous system such as that produced by excessive masturbation or very frequent nocturnal emissions."[4] Stekel doubted that neurasthenia differed from Freud's "psychoneurosis" by reason of its immediate somatic etiology and claimed that the effects of complexes are evident in actual neuroses. Freud's position concerning this was that "the above-mentioned forms of neurosis do occasionally occur alone; more frequently, however, they combine with one another or with a psychoneurotic affect . . ." He stated that in normal and neurotic individuals it is not a question of whether these complexes and conflicts exist but rather "whether they have become pathogenic, and if so, which mechanisms they have laid claim to."[5]

[4] *Three Contributions to the Theory of Sex.*
[5] *Die Onanie* (Wiesbaden, 1912).

At the time, Stekel suspected the correct interconnections but, in the question of actual neurosis, fell into the error he would repeat later in his examination of epilepsy. He deduced a causal interpretation from the mere existence of the diverse drive impulses, without asking himself *specifically* how the impulses cause the various aspects of the disease.

It is advisable here to differentiate between two major categories of neurasthenia. *Acute neurasthenia* appears suddenly and may in some cases be cured or alleviated through remedying certain impairments to the patient's sexual life in full accord with Freudian concepts. Some of the symptoms not present here are characteristic of *chronic* (hypochondriacal) *neurasthenia:*[6] chronic constipation (usually from early childhood on), flatulence, nausea, lack of appetite, constant headache, ejaculatio praecox without erection, ante portas, seepage of urine, or spermatorrhea. These symptoms appear only sporadically in the acute form and are not very pronounced; they appear when the damage has become chronic.

Regarding the origin of neurasthenia, we must determine whether wish fantasies find their distorted expression directly in the symptoms, as in hysteria or compulsion neurosis, or whether psychic inhibitions they create are the result of a conflict-laden drive constellation and contribute indirectly to bringing about the illness. We anticipate that the first possibility corresponds to the chronic form of neurasthenia and the second to the acute. In this section we shall discuss only the latter.

In screening data gathered through brief anamnesis, one encounters both confirmations of and exceptions to the Freudian concept of neurasthenia. For example, the causal connection between masturbation or nocturnal

---

[6] *Cf.* Reich, "Über die chronische hypochondrische Neurasthenie," *Internationale Zeitschrift für Psychoanalyse*, XII, 1926.

emissions and neurasthenia seems confirmed by some
cases, while in others, symptoms appeared only after suppression of masturbation. Indeed, although one often
hears of masturbation being replaced by frequent emissions during the night or day, and although some patients
masturbate excessively (i.e., several times a day), compulsively, and with little satisfaction, two facts seem to
contradict Freud's assumption: first, some patients
manifest the neurasthenic constellation of symptoms
despite infrequent masturbation or infrequent nocturnal
emissions; second, there are cases of excessive masturbation in which the patient never suffers from the symptoms
of neurasthenia.

A few examples of different reactions to masturbation
or to sexual intercourse will help us gain a more precise
orientation.

*Case 1: Acute neurasthenia with excessive mas-
turbation.* A twenty-two-year-old student had been
masturbating for a number of years, two or three times a
day, with vivid rape fantasies, which were accompanied
by guilt feelings and remorse. For several months he had
suffered from great restlessness, depression, inability to
work and think, as well as backaches and general fatigue;
he experienced no irritability, no constipation, no
headaches, no spermatorrhea. Coitus was not attempted,
due to his disgust toward women. Masturbation was
characterized by rhythmical manual stimulation of the
penis and rhythmical seminal discharge. In the eighth session the patient recognized his mother in the woman he
fantasized, a realization triggered by a certain detail.
After I explained to him that his disgust for women was
probably related to incestuous desire, the patient visited a
prostitute and had intercourse three times with full
satisfaction. His symptoms disappeared completely; he re-

mained potent for the time being and discontinued treatment after a few more sessions. Some months later he returned, again because of continual depression and work dissatisfaction. However, he was capable of working and masturbated very rarely; he had ceased having intercourse with prostitutes. The other previous symptoms had not returned. External circumstances rendered the continuation of treatment impracticable.

Here we have a truly classic case of Freudian neurasthenia, manifesting a psychoneurotic basis (an incestuous fixation). The permanent remission of the neurasthenic symptoms following curtailment of masturbation and commencement of satisfying sexual intercourse confirmed the hypothesis. This was a case of *acute* neurasthenia without the characteristic symptoms of the chronic form, that is, obstipation, headaches, spermatorrhea, and ejaculatio praecox. Masturbation was genital; it was stimulated by fantasies of coitus.

Case 2: Mild acute neurasthenia without masturbation. A young physician complained of great irritability, impatience, restlessness, and mild depression, which had become noticeable over a two-year period. He was potent and had intercourse on an average of one to three times every three weeks, each time with a different woman. However, he was not satisfied by intercourse and prolonged foreplay. Ejaculation usually occurred after four to eight thrusts. The climax curve was flat, lacking the sudden steep decline. During coitus he was disturbed by the thought that his penis was too small for him to be able to satisfy the woman. This feeling was much more pronounced in relation to married women than to maidens. He always assumed that the wives had big, strong husbands with whom he could not compare. Furthermore, he practiced coitus interruptus. Some discussion and the use of suggestion eliminated his self-doubts, and the symptoms eased.

From this case we may conclude that it was not erective or ejaculative potency but only orgastic potency that was disturbed by inhibitory ideas.

The next case demonstrates that neurasthenic symptoms may also result from abstinence. This is utterly confusing because, according to Freud, we would expect not neurasthenia but anxiety neurosis.

Case 3: Acute neurasthenia with abstinence. A thirty-six-year-old woman in treatment for bronchial asthma had become ill three years prior to treatment, following a miscarriage. Thereafter, in anger, she had refused her lover and remained almost completely abstinent. She had always been vaginally anesthetic and could be satisfied only through clitoral cunnilingus. The following symptoms had existed for about two years: fatigue, extreme irritability, depression, and physical distress such as a "leaden heaviness" in the legs and backaches. In analysis the immediate conflict was sufficiently solved that she was again able to achieve her usual satisfaction. The symptoms promptly disappeared. They reappeared several times after periods of prolonged abstinence due to heightened conflicts, but receded once again following satisfaction through cunnilingus. In contrast to the asthma, these symptoms were not accessible to psychological interpretation. However, it was characteristic for the asthma, as well, to improve after gratification and worsen during abstinence.

Case 4: Excessive masturbation without neurasthenia. A thirty-two-year-old male homosexual had begun to masturbate at age six, and from puberty had masturbated almost daily one to three times, occasionally even more often. Aside from erective impotence with women, with no ejaculatio praecox, and homosexuality, there were no symptoms whatsoever. The patient had no appreciable depression; on the contrary, he was slightly hypomanic, self-confident, a prototype of the narcissistic homosexual. Masturbation fantasies were bisexual and satisfied him. He enjoyed masturbating and had no inhibitions or conscious guilt feelings about doing it. Treatment led to complete and lasting success after one year. (I followed the case for six years.) The patient no longer masturbated or had homosexual desires, was fully potent, and capable of loving.

Case 5: Excessive masturbation without neurasthenia. A twenty-year-old man sought treatment for premature ejaculation, blushing, and spells of nervousness. He had been homosexually active for a time, inclined to boasting, and had masturbated almost daily from age eight, often three times in immediate succession. He did not display neurasthenic symptoms. Masturbation fantasies were genital-heterosexual and occasionally also active-homosexual. Masturbation was completely satisfying, not accompanied by guilt, and therefore relinquished during analysis only with the greatest effort. Although guilt feelings were not connected with masturbation, they were predominantly anchored in characterological idiosyncrasies. Analysis ended in complete success after ten months. In a review of the case one year later, there was no evidence of relapse.

The last two cases demonstrate that only masturbation that is directly disturbed by guilt feelings causes neurasthenia. The inhibitory effects of guilt on the tendency toward sexual satisfaction are directly manifested in the modification and impeding of the stimulus-discharge. Satisfaction dissipates, preventing the reduction of sexual tension. It is of decisive significance whether remorse is felt only after masturbation, or during it, undermining the pleasure experience. Reports of masturbators indicate that some individuals momentarily overcome their scruples, achieve satisfaction as far as this is possible in the autoerotic act, and afterward are seized by remorse. In such cases guilt is unable to affect the course of the pleasure experience and the release of tension because it has been momentarily eliminated. When scruples and inhibitions set in *during* masturbation, however, the result is psychic disturbance of the physiological stimulus-discharge, a faltering of pleasure, and no steep drop in the orgasm. A greater or lesser accumulation of excitation remains undischarged, producing somatic disturbances. This would explain why abstinence or renouncement of masturbation occasionally results not in anxiety neurosis but in neurasthenia, which includes among its symptoms hypochondriacal sensations.

Unquestionably, a disturbance of the stimulus-discharge process actually implies an irritation of the vegetative nervous system due to the blocking of a reflex reaction. The residue of unreleased vegetative excitation plays the leading role in excessive masturbation as its motor force. Patients who masturbate without guilt are at least relieved of their physical tension, feel well afterward, and do not think of masturbation for a time. The more ambivalent the pleasure experience during masturbation, the more noticeable the somatic, and the psychic, disturbances become. At one time Ferenczi thought that "it is possible that the wave of pleasure normally ebbs away completely, but in masturbation part of the excitation cannot be properly released; this remaining amount could explain one-day neurasthenia, and perhaps even neurasthenia itself."[7] Obviously, this dynamic would apply only in cases of conflict-ridden masturbation, otherwise anyone who masturbates would become neurasthenic. Very frequently individuals suffer no harm from masturbation until guilt feelings and anxiety develop due to unrestrained fantasy or prurient literature and lead to neurasthenia.

Loveless intercourse also occasionally leads to neurasthenia, because the conflict of attitudes disturbs the stimulus-discharge process. In this context Tausk's observation is correct. He found guilt feelings only "where masturbation did not afford full satisfaction and fear developed. On the other hand, I was able to see that no guilt feelings were attached to masturbation which yielded full pleasure." His interpretation of this observation is erroneous, however. It should be reversed: masturbation produces full pleasure when it is free of guilt feelings.

Thus, acute neurasthenia has a direct physical and an indirect psychic foundation. A disturbing psychic inhibition is always present, otherwise the organism would find full satisfaction.

What has been said about the reduction of orgastic potency and the dispersion of orgasm in men holds equally true for women who are vaginally anesthetic and masturbate clitorally. They have rejected and repressed the female sexual role. But physical female characteristics (lack of a penis, menstruation) contradict their conscious or unconscious masculinity desires and make sexual gratification all the less possible, despite occasional, relatively full orgastic release of physical tension. After an extended period of masturbation, guilt feelings tend to

[7] *Versuch einer Genitaltheorie*, Internationale Psychoanalytische Bibliothek, Nr. XV. Internationaler Psychoanalytischer Verlag, 1924.

arise, inducing consequences of the disturbed stimulus-discharge process described above.

Total Orgastic Impotence

In men this is found only in connection with ejaculative impotence and genital asthenia; in neurotic women it is always present.

In Figure 7 I have shown two typical, basic forms of vaginal hypesthesia with orgastic impotence (curves *b* and *c*) and the nonpleasure reaction of the frigid woman (curve *a*).

Curve *b* represents the disturbance of sensation in which vaginal excitation is low at the outset and hardly rises during coitus. Curve *c* represents a different form of this disorder: vaginal excitability is initially unimpaired. Excitation builds steadily until the moment the phase of involuntary muscle contractions should begin. Suddenly, excitation subsides or simply dissipates without an orgasm. This form of orgastic impotence usually replaces total insensitivity (anesthesia) as soon as the most important inhibitions concerning coitus have been removed. It poses the most interesting problems in regard to female genitality and its removal (which is, after all, the aim in treating frigidity) is far more difficult than the elimination of the anesthesia. Since achievement of vaginal orgastic potency in nonabstinent women is to be regarded as the most important indication of successful treatment, it requires further consideration.

Female orgastic potency is dependent upon, among other factors, male erective potency. For example, vaginally sensitive women with orgastic potency may not reach end satisfaction if the man has already ejaculated.

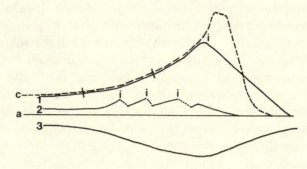

FIGURE 7. *Typical forms of frigidity*

    c. line of comparison
    1. normal vaginal sensitivity with
        isolated orgasmic impotence
    2. vaginal hypesthesia
    a. no excitation
    3. nonpleasure with total frigidity
    i. inhibition prior to the phase of
       involuntary muscle contractions

They are disturbed by the thought that the penis will now "go soft" and they will not be able to achieve satisfaction. Sometimes this idea manifests itself at the outset of the act; the woman is possessed by the thought that she "must hurry," otherwise she will be "too late to climax." She makes a great effort and, precisely because she does not simply surrender to her sensations, her excitation does not increase, not even when the male erection lasts for some time after ejaculation. Typically, the excitation of such women subsides the moment male orgasm begins. Careful analysis reveals that at this moment they are seized by a strange curiosity and observe both themselves and the man.

While engaged in coitus inversus, an impulsive, totally frigid female psychopath bit her husband in the larynx during his orgasm, whereupon he fainted. In analysis she reported having often fantasized that a woman could achieve greatest satisfaction by castrating the man during his orgasm. Thoughts that were fully conscious in this case are unconscious in women suffering from the orgasm disturbance described above. During coitus the woman identifies with the man and fantasizes that his penis belongs to her. When the penis becomes flaccid, she fantasizes that her *own* pleasure-giving organ is being taken from her and, hence, that she is being genitally injured. Simultaneously, castration impulses toward the man, which were already present, are fulfilled. She remains excited as long as nothing interferes with her fantasy of being a man. She loses her excitement—in more exact terms, she renounces her vaginal excitement—when she is to lose the penis that she has "borrowed." The disturbing idea of not being able to achieve satisfaction originates in the unconscious fear of not being able to keep the penis.

The most frequent cause of orgastic impotence in women is *fear of orgastic excitation.* Only rarely is this inhibition as superficial as it is in the following case. A female patient was unable to achieve an orgasm because her husband had once laughed during her climax—it was the first time she had had orgastic sensations—and afterward asked, "Were you in seventh heaven?" The memory of this decidedly insensitive behavior had inhibited her ever since, and she was able to have intercourse only unwillingly and without enjoyment. She withdrew into infantile satisfactions, and when she no longer allowed herself these, succumbed to an anxiety hysteria.

In some cases, fear of defecating or urinating during the orgasm prevents a climax. In women the idea of coitus is associated with defecation from earliest childhood. In the unconscious emotional life the vagina is the same as the anus. Orgastic excitation stimulates sensations of defecating. The connection between anxiety affect and sexual satisfaction is expressed most clearly in the fact that children normally react to frightening experiences as well as to sexual excitation with bladder and intestinal urgency.

A good example of this was offered by a female patient who, at the moment her orgasm was to begin, would be beset by fear fantasies that made her unable to retain her urine or flatus. Because of embarrassment and fear, genital excitation could not be sustained and she became an insomniac.

The analysis of a female patient suffering from chronic hypochondriacal neurasthenia yielded information concerning the source of such an inhibition of the orgasm. In one of her masochistic masturbation fantasies the patient was stripped, chained, and locked in a cage, where she was allowed to starve. At this point the inhibition of the orgasm occurred. Suddenly she felt constrained to brood about a machine that could automatically remove the feces and urine of the chained girl "who is not allowed to move" (instead of being "unable to move"). The following dream occurred during this period:

[Part 1]: From a friendly and likeable person I have turned into a wicked, fierce, stubborn, and horrible creature. Afterward, it all changed and I told Grandpa it was his fault because of the fingers [or something like that]. He replied, "I didn't know an amputated penis"—[he meant "finger"]—"could go into the character"[or in the anus or intestines].

[Part 2]: In the vicinity of K. [a summer resort visited at age three or four], I am lying in a truck, almost as if I were in bed; I am between two automobiles which want to come together. I am afraid they will squash my car and

I will be buried underneath and suffocate. One swerves to the left and I am afraid they will collide in the back, that something will happen in back.

One year of analytic work had enabled her to understand her masochism. For example, her fantasizing during puberty that her lover forced her to submit to numerous men and be beaten by them in a brothel was her way of excusing herself to her conscience for her own desire for intercourse; after all, she was forced, therefore she was innocent. Because it contained overt coitus, she finally renounced this disguised fantasy, as well, and masturbated only with pregenital masochistic fantasies, such as being beaten with a wire broom and then having salt and pepper rubbed into the wounds; having nails pounded into her flesh; or being forced to eat, naked, from a feeding trough, with chained hands (masturbation prohibition), while being smeared with feces from head to toe. In analysis, undisguised masochistic coitus fantasies reappeared, and she recognized in her genital anxiety her motives for escaping to pregenital satisfaction. The dream brought back the situation in which she had experienced this anxiety in connection with the fear of defecation.

The patient associated a "marshy woods" with the story of little Eyolf, who drowned in a pond while his parents were having intercourse. The "two automobiles which want to come together" are her parents; she is lying in between "almost as if I were in bed." While writing down the partially analyzed dream, the patient added of her own accord:

I once heard in a lecture that masturbation makes the small labia grow larger. At the time, I was afraid it would happen to me and they would notice everything. "Two amputated fingers" means both labia grown long and squashed by being "run over." In the story of "little Eyolf," Ibsen complains not only that children are allowed to sleep in the parents' bedroom but, furthermore (as happened to me, at least in my dream), that when a child is present, you must no longer have intercourse with each other and must not treat the child as a matter of secondary importance because something could "happen" to me. Finally, there is only the danger of something happening "in back." (And these incessant stomach aches and intestinal troubles! I had flatulence just the night before, by the way, and wondered whether this was also related to our present analysis of coitus fear?) Both parents should pay attention to me and not to each other, that is why I am in the middle. Grandpa is probably laughing because he is naked and urinating proudly (not seen in the dream!). He is standing there like the boy I saw in Votiv Park the day before.

For a better understanding of the connection between the dream and the fantasy of lying in a cage, naked, chained, and hungry, we shall report a different dream, which occurred two days earlier: "I am sitting on a stool in the kitchen. Before me there is a cage with two birds which I am observing carefully, as if I had to see something before I operate on them. I am thinking that one does not do that in public. Dim lights." In connection with this she recalled an anxiety dream from early childhood: "Something is happening to Mother— she is having an operation."

Several days before, she had read the word *vögeln** in a book by Fliess. The cage represented her crib. "One does not do that in public" pertains to flatus and defecation. For many years the patient had avoided all social gatherings because, on several occasions, she had passed a

* This is the slang word for "to have intercourse," and also associates aurally with the word *Vogel*, "bird." [Trans.]

"*malheur* from behind" in the presence of men she liked and had gotten diarrhea. In analysis, as well, she would experience uncontrollable urinary and intestinal urgency when sexual feelings developed in connection with transference. When she became aware that the masochistic fantasies represented fear-laden coitus, normal coitus fantasies without fear appeared with transference. However, shortly before orgasm was to occur, the masochistic fantasies reemerged. Fear of coitus had been eliminated. Anxiety was now restricted to the fear of orgasm.

Based on the facts mentioned above, I arrived at the following reconstruction of the primal scene. While lying next to her parents, the patient had been overpowered ("chained") by the fear they might notice her observing them in the act of coitus; hence she dared not move. The sexual excitation, mingled with fear, expressed itself in urinary and intestinal distress, and she yearned for a machine to remove the waste unnoticed. The physical and mental torture that the child suffered at the time remained permanently associated with sexual pleasure and had caused fixation of the masochistic masturbation fantasies. The sadistic conception of coitus and the genital anxiety had been mainly responsible for this; the latter, in particular, was her motivation for escape from the dangers of genital activity into the realm of anal masochism.

Another female patient suffering from hypochondriacal anxiety was vaginally anesthetic prior to analysis. Analysis first eliminated that part of her genital anxiety which had expressed itself as vaginismus. She developed vaginal sensitivity and a conscious desire for sexual satisfaction, but could not achieve an orgasm. Just before it was to occur, it would "break off." Analysis revealed that in masturbation she had forbidden herself end pleasure as harmful. In this context she reported the following dream:

> I dreamed of a tower of rough red tiles which had a slight ledge on the wall, barely large enough for a toe hold. I climbed around the outside toward the top and, when I had only a short way to go, the tile I was holding on to with my left hand came loose. I was overcome with fear; how horrible to be so high up—if I lose my grasp, I'll be killed. I would rather walk the long way back and feel as if you* are watching me. I want to show you that I'm brave, but I am glad that my husband suddenly appears and is walking ahead of me. If my husband doesn't fall off, then I will just jump off quickly and you will see how brave I am. My husband does jump off, but I am afraid to do the same.

We shall emphasize only the elements relevant to our theme. The slight ledge on the wall is the clitoris. She is climbing "around," that is, past, the clitoris, "upward" (this represents an attempt to masturbate vaginally). Despite her protestations, certain of the patient's behavioral patterns proved that she had not yet entirely overcome her fear of masturbation. She was indeed able to discuss the infantile and pubertal masturbation she had practiced until the onset of her illness and had long concealed from the analyst, but she shrank from the thought that she could ever masturbate again. This indicated that the desire to masturbate had not been eliminated but, rather, had been repressed. Progress in overcoming this repression was long in coming, in spite of ample proof that she was struggling against actual masturbation wishes. For this reason I told her one day that I did not believe her

* I.e., Reich. [Trans.]

claim that she was now convinced masturbation was unharmful and was no longer afraid of it; that I was sure she would not allow herself to masturbate if a desire to were to become conscious. She insisted that she no longer either feared such wishes or had them. In the next session she reported the dream I have just described. The tile came loose while she was still "high up" that is, before orgasm occurred ("when I had only a short way to go"), and she was afraid of falling and being killed. (The patient had entered analysis because she was afraid of dying of tuberculosis; during puberty she had thought that masturbation, and particularly orgasm, caused lung disease.) She wanted to show me she was brave enough to masturbate, but was relieved when her husband arrived and climbed up with her, that is, had intercourse with her. Sexual excitation would always "break off" when her husband's orgasm occurred. ("If my husband doesn't fall off," etc.). However, she could not achieve an orgasm even when her husband did not ejaculate too soon. She was afraid of the orgasm itself, which she portrayed as "falling down." Once, when she had experienced a sensation similar to orgasm during masturbation, she thought she was "going to die." Another patient, who was completely cured of her frigidity by analysis and was subsequently only rarely orgastically impotent, told me later that when this sensation occurred, it was as if she were continually climbing upward and did not dare "jump down." A female schizoid psychopath reported the same thing.[8]

If the orgasm is disturbed by anxiety, orgastic release of tension is experienced as falling. This may be one of the

[8] These case histories date from the first efforts to apply a character-analytic technique. In the years 1922–1925 this differed from the Freudian psychoanalytic technique only by reason of an exact examination of genital disturbances.

reasons why dreams of falling so frequently represent genital anxiety and impotence. Many individuals experience sensations of both anxiety and pleasure in the genitals when they look down from a high place or just imagine themselves falling from a great height. One also experiences simultaneous anxiety and pleasure sensations in the genitals and the heart on swings, in quickly descending elevators, in automobiles speeding downhill, and on skis, racing down a steep slope. These sensations have a very specific quality, for example, "my heart sank" (in the vernacular, "my heart fell into my trousers"), "something is being lost." Some people feel "pulling in the genitals." Sensations of fear are experienced at the root of the penis. The physiological basis of the symbolic equation: heart—genitals (fear—pleasure) will occupy us in detail in the following sections.

A female patient with suicidal tendencies fantasized throwing herself out of a window[9] and being caught in the arms of God. Analysis exposed this idea as an incest fantasy. When asked why she was unable to achieve satisfaction in masturbation, the patient replied that she had the frightening sensation of falling out of a window from a very great height; hence, the same idea as in the suicide fantasy.

An hysterical male patient with hypochondriacal fear of catastrophe had already overcome his fear and sexual timidity in analysis. During analysis of infantile masturbation, to which the last traces of his castration anxiety were attached, he had the following anxiety dream, in which the orgasm was unmistakably represented as a fall (loss, castration):

[9] In dreams the predominant significance of falling is either birth or orgasm, according to the libido position. The patient fluctuates between striving for genital satisfaction, which frightens him, and the intrauterine situation, which is to protect him from the dangers of sexual satisfaction.

A young, handsome man is high in the mountains. There is a storm, and he appears to have lost his way. A skeletal hand (death) has taken him by the arm and seems to be leading him (apparently, a symbol that he is doomed). A man and a little boy fall off a cliff. At the same time a rucksack loses its contents; the boy is surrounded by whitish ooze.

The first part of the dream contains fear of the consequences of masturbation. His fear of catastrophe (having to die, going insane) had appeared after a visit to a hygiene exhibition where he had seen syphilitic sores. The "little boy" in the second part of the dream represents both himself and his genitalia. During the fall, his rucksack (testes) loses its contents (ejaculation), and the boy (penis) is surrounded with whitish ooze (sperm, allusion to syphilitic sores).

The feeling of "losing something" or of "losing oneself" is closely tied to orgasm and is based directly on the sudden loss of sexual tension connected with expulsion of semen in men and profuse vaginal secretion in women. Nevertheless, the particular feeling of "losing something" may very well stem from castration anxiety, which causes the orgasm to be experienced as a genital danger. Support for this position comes from those cases in which persons fear the orgasm as a powerful sensation that overcomes and controls them, throwing them into confusion and clouding consciousness. This sensation was first experienced during masturbation; perhaps the experience was frightening and later led to the idea that loss of semen and the physical paroxysm shatter the nerves. Thus, in addition to infantile castration anxiety, which is further heightened by pornographic literature, there is the physical sensation of the orgasm. Because of present-day morals, it is at first experienced with anxiety. In patients who do not shun stimulation of the genitals but deny themselves orgasm, it must therefore be assumed that genital anxiety has become dominant primarily from the upsetting experience of the first orgasm. Therapy in such cases must be directed at removing the fear of masturbation. Such patients must be able to masturbate without anxiety.

Regarding the problem of anxiety at the moment of orgasm, simply analyzing the anxiety ideation is, in many cases, not enough. At the transition to the climax, anxiety causes many women's coital movements to become erratic. Here an elucidation of sexual technique is usually indispensable. If, at first by conscious and deliberate practice, the woman overcomes her inhibition, the first orgastic experience will follow automatically. This, in turn, will help to remove the last remnants of anxiety. However, clinical experience has shown emphatically that treatment of the anxiety is merely the necessary preliminary. Completion of the cure is always brought about only by actual sexual experience. I shall return in detail to issues of therapy in the last part of this book.

Sexual Excitation in Nymphomania

Figure 8 depicts the course of excitation in women who suffer greatly from the fact that they experience sensations similar to climax a number of times during intercourse but cannot achieve release of tension and thus remain in a state of constant sexual excitation ("nymphomania"). Incessant desire for intercourse and a craving for many men are frequently the direct consequences of this form of orgastic impotence.

From the outset, excitation in the nymphomaniac is

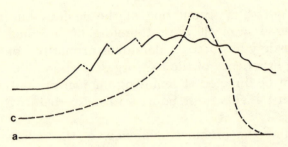

FIGURE 8.   *Nymphomaniacal sexual excitation*
—repeated increase of tension with no final release

a. no excitation
c. line of comparison

considerably higher than in orgastically potent people and also increases much faster during intercourse; it evaporates partially at the height of tension, but the orgastic flow of excitation back into the body does not take place. Thus, inhibition occurs only *after* excitation has been focused on the genitals.

CHAPTER FOUR

Sexual Stasis: The Energy Source of Neurosis

The fact that the hidden meaning and purpose of a symptom, which appears meaningless when viewed superficially, can be deduced from the associations connected with it, does not allow conclusions to be drawn regarding the source from which the symptom derives its energy. A symptom may—but need not—disappear when its hidden meaning and purpose have become conscious; it can be finally eliminated only when the source of its energy has been withdrawn. Only withdrawal of the energy from the root of the symptom formation can be termed radical therapy. Thus, in every neurotic symptom the following aspects should be distinguished:

1. *Psychic meaning.* Since Freud, this has meant, in the simplest terms, those repressed ideas, experiences, desires, satisfactions, self-punitive acts, and so forth, that achieve disguised expression in the symptom. But these psychic elements would not be able to create symptoms if they were not charged with dammed-up drive energy. Most of the repressed ideas that emerge as significant components

in the analysis of a neurotic symptom are secondary additions to an already established symptom. This can be seen by merely comparing the cross section of the symptom with its development. In their writings, many therapists who neither accept the sexual etiology of neuroses nor concern themselves with the infantile roots of a symptom constantly confuse the meaning of a symptom with its etiology, and are consequently unable to find any of the specific mechanisms. Again and again, in every mental illness, they discover "complexes" that are already known and use them to "explain" the illness, ignoring the objection that the important thing is to eliminate the source of energy at the root of the illness.

2. *Purpose.* Apart from serving as an energy outlet, the chief purpose of the symptom may be defined as the so-called secondary gain from illness, which more or less explicitly dominates the picture in every neurosis. Once the neurosis has evolved as the result of pathological conflict solution, the symptom is used by the patient to achieve certain goals which, without exception, are intimately related to its causes. This tendency of the symptom is the consequence, never the primary cause, of the neurosis. However, secondarily, it complicates and aggravates the neurotic conflict and in many cases totally obscures the primary causes of the conflict. Adler's exclusively outcome-oriented "individual psychology" views these tendencies of the neurotic will and the "fictitious goals" toward which it strives as the essentials of neurosis, paying no attention to its sex-economic function.

3. *Energy source.* Inquiry into the nature of the real causes of a psychic illness necessitates going beyond the experience that has become pathogenic, and beyond the additional secondary goals of a neurosis, to the very limit of

psychologically understandable drive activity. This activity is subject to biological laws and is predominantly rooted in physiological processes occurring in the realm of vegetative energy regulation.

Let me illustrate with an analogy what I see as being the energy source of psychic illness, as distinct from its psychic functions, purposes, historical foundations, and so on. This distinction is indispensable if one is to understand how neuroses are cured by the release of energy and its withdrawal. It also clearly separates the sex-economic view of psychic illness from all other views, which are concerned only with unconscious content and meaning or childhood origins.

The strength, shape, and breadth of a river system are determined chiefly by its sources. If the springs are plentiful, and lie high in the mountains, and if, perhaps, there are glaciers, the stream will develop a stronger flow, a swifter current, and will build up more energy than if the sources are meager and located in flat land. What is important about a river in terms of natural science, is not whether it can take barges or only small boats, nor whether it winds five times or ten, nor whether it divides at its mouth into two or into eight branches, nor whether it is ten miles long or a hundred. All these characteristics depend fundamentally on only two factors: the abundance and strength of the springs and the shape of the terrain through which the streams must make their way. The amount of power that can be harnessed, the number of bends in the river, the width of the riverbed and its navigability, indeed, everything else is conditioned by those two factors and their relation to each other. If the amount of water flowing off through the river system always corresponds to the amount issuing from the springs, then the energy of the fall will always equalize. No more flows in than can flow out. To a certain degree the conditions of the outflow can be altered: confined by dams, regulated by locks, facilitated by widening the riverbed. The energy of the current may be infinitely exploited without any danger—under one condition: that the balance of energy be maintained; that the same amount of water always flows out as flows in.

But the moment one tries to make use of the current by obstructing or perhaps even totally preventing the outflow, the natural self-regulation of the energy exchange will be disturbed. If a dam were to block the riverbed, water would flood over the banks. The difference between the amount of water flowing in and the amount flowing out would create a new, artificial force that could no longer be regulated and utilized as had the original energy flow, the equalization of which had been assured. The more complete the closure of the outflow, the greater the disruption in the surrounding area, and the smaller the chance of controlling it. If new dams were to be made to curb the water now overflowing the riverbanks, still more power would accumulate, and the danger would increase a hundredfold. By the law of the conservation of energy, each new dam would only succeed in achieving, increasingly, the very opposite of what was intended. There are, then, only two possibilities: destroy the sources of the flow—an impossible undertaking—or remove the dam, which was originally built on a false assumption, thus restoring the flow to its old channels, and make use of its energy while totally securing the equalization between inflow and outflow.

This example may be applied directly to the energy flow of sexuality. The source of this flow cannot be destroyed, since that would entail the destruction of the vegetative function, that is, death itself. Building an ever increasing number of dams against its flow would only foster the emergence of uncontrollable, unnatural, and destructive forces. Regarding the flow of the sexual current, the first axiom is, again, inflow and outflow must be equalized. However, in this case it must be expressed another way. Instead of inflow, we must refer to energy build-up or tension; instead of outflow, energy discharge, release, or satisfaction.

The energy produced by the central vegetative apparatus corresponds to the water that flows from the springs. The vegetative energy source determines the intensity of an individual's sexuality; the structure of society determines the outlets sexuality can find and the release it is allowed. For this reason we must make a fundamental distinction between a balanced and an unbalanced sex (*energy*) economy. The diagram of the former shows that the amount of energy discharge is equal to that of energy accumulation.

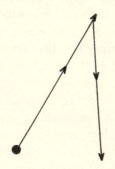

The diagram of an unbalanced sex economy always shows a discrepancy between tension and release. The tension may be greater than the release, but the release can never be greater than the tension.

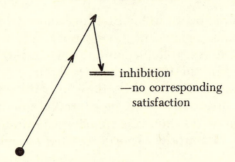

The disturbances of genital functioning (impotence and frigidity in their manifold forms) thus represent the dams that prevent the orderly equalization of sexual energy in human beings. They are created by a sexual upbringing that deadens sexuality in the infant and are the direct cause of all forms of psychic illness, including psychosis, perversion, and neurotic criminality.

In the almost twenty years of my very extensive practice as a psychotherapist, I have never seen a case of neurosis, antisocial pathology, criminality, psychosis, or perversion without at least some impairment of orgastic function. Orgastic disturbance is thus the key to an understanding of the energy economy of every such illness. Neuroses are nothing but the attempts of the organism to compensate for the disturbance in the energy equilibrium.

What is the relation between the disturbance of genital functioning and the neurotic process? In the case of psychoneurosis this is not hard to answer. Whatever the level of psychic development at which the neurotic conflict sets in, repression always includes the genital strivings, cutting them off more or less completely from the motor force. To this end, every kind of function-inhibiting mechanism found in the various forms of neurosis may be invoked. Inhibition of the genital function then induces sexual stasis, which, in turn, intensifies the psychic conflict, complicating and consolidating it.

It seems evident that *psychic conflict, in itself non-pathological, becomes neurotic conflict with all the attendant consequences only when sexual stasis is added to it,* that is, as soon as the energy source for the symptom formation has been created. Repression of an instinctual impulse does not in itself create a symptom; rather, a symptom arises as soon as the stasis becomes so great that the instinctual impulse succeeds in breaking through the repression imposed by the defending ego. The physical tensions and sensations peculiar to neurasthenia, anxiety neurosis, or hypochondria are always present at the outset of a neurotic illness and are the direct expression of the vegetative-sexual stasis. Furthermore, there is always a time lapse between the repression of the drive and the symptom formation; its length is determined by the degree of disturbance of the genital function. This may be seen particularly clearly, for instance, in erythrophobia. The patient fights against masturbation for months or for years; finally he succeeds in repressing it entirely. The social shyness that had existed previously at first diminishes, becoming noticeably stronger again only when, weeks or months later, and in connection with innocuous everyday matters, blushing appears for the first time with all its stasis-neurotic concomitants.

The causal connections between neurosis and sexual stasis are most clearly evidenced in sexual-stasis neuroses.

The Symptoms of Sexual Stasis

The typical symptoms of illness caused by sexual stasis are heart ailments (asystole, tachycardia, arrhythmias, extrasystoles, etc.), excessive perspiration, hot flashes and chills, trembling, dizziness, diarrhea, and, occasionally, increased salivation. It is particularly noteworthy that whereas in some cases these symptoms have a hidden psychic meaning and purpose, in others they do not (unless psychic content is willfully read into them) and are simply the expression of a general vegetative overexcitation. Even when they do have some psychic meaning, the symptoms perfectly obey the natural laws of conversion hysteria described by Freud. Thus, blushing in erythrophobia signifies social shame connected with masturbation. In terms of energy, blushing is the result of dammed-up sexual energy being displaced upward to the head instead of to the genitals.

If we adhere to our classifications of *meaning, purpose,* and *source* of the symptom, the differences as well as the similarities between vasomotor neuroses with hysterical mechanisms and those without become clear. Common to both is the fact that the organs in which pathological symptoms appear are governed by the vegetative nervous system. In the case of anxiety hysteria, this system becomes charged with the blocked energy that results from the repression of affectively charged ideas. The vulnerability of any given organ in the system is determined by its vegetative excitability. In hysterical vasoneurosis, genital energies are supplied to the vasovegetative nervous system. Blushing may signify an act of genital exhibitionism, and trembling of the head may represent masturbation or castration. Hot flashes are very frequently revealed in analysis to be the expression of physical genital excitation which is not allowed to become conscious; diarrhea may be an expression of anxiety or sexual excitation. Some patients who are unable to achieve erection when attempting intercourse perspire excessively. Here, as a result of the displacement of excitation, the energy is directed to the skin of the rest of the body instead of to the penis.

Does psychic identification cause the sudden perspiration? Does an unconscious desire to return to the womb perhaps produce the "erection" at the skin's surface? Certainly such cannot be the case. It is conceivable only that the vegetative excitation that produced the desire for coitus is not allowed to reach the genitals, due to psychic inhibitions or anxiety, and thus seizes upon the sweat glands. The blocked excitation is then directed by the ideational content, which we find upon dissecting the symptom, toward an appropriate erogenous organ. The same holds true for hot flashes. They are originally caused by sexual excitation and are filled with sexual ideation, even if the sexual excitation is not perceived as such. Since sensations of heat also accompany normal sexual excitation, the physiological process cannot be considered a conversion symptom. Only the missing perception of genital sensation is pathological.

Some hysterical patients experience chills in place of sexual excitation or anxiety. A female patient who frequently felt genitally excited during her sessions experienced chills every time the doctor rejected her. The psychic meaning of the chills was the desire to be warmed by the analyst as by a mother, but the patient was able to express this only after her sexual excitation had been replaced by anxiety, which was revealed in the response of the skin.

The symptoms of vasomotor neurosis expressing an irritation of the vegetative nervous system may be induced by various causes. For example, Basedow's disease,* a thyroid dysfunction, produces the same symptoms that in moments of danger appear as expressions and concomitants of fright. However, as the starting point of our investigation, we shall first take a simpler phenomenon—the symptoms of nicotine poisoning.

*Exophthalmic goiter. [Trans.]

Here self-observation shows that the first indication of nicotine poisoning is a brief interruption of heartbeat followed by an accelerated heartbeat. At the moment the heart stops, anxiety appears, followed later by vertigo, nausea, and perspiration. The anxiety which originally was without mental content now gradually becomes associated with a fear of dying, which is based on the rational consideration that nicotine abuse may cause coronary disease and, hence, premature death. The longer the palpitation continues and the more intense it becomes, the stronger the fear of death, until it reaches panic proportions and secondarily aggravates the cardiac symptoms. The sequence in which the symptoms appear corresponds entirely to those which occur in a vasomotor neurosis: the nicotinism takes hold of the vegetative nervous system; this irritation is the chief cause of the tachycardia and later of the general symptoms as well. The tachycardia is accompanied by anxiety without content, which, secondarily, combines with the fear of death. For the moment only the combination of cardiac arrhythmia and tachycardia with free-floating anxiety is of interest to our problem of stasis neurotic anxiety.

Free-floating anxiety is the expression of a particular type of vegetative irritation affecting the cardiac and respiratory functions. If, in place of nicotine, we now imagine a quantity of sexual excitation that has not been physiologically discharged, we can clearly see the etiology of sexual-stasis anxiety. The irritation of the vegetative system caused by sexual stasis is revealed in the form of cardiac anxiety, which is always at the core of anxiety neurosis. As in nicotine poisoning, Basedow's disease, and angina pectoris, the anxiety arises directly from cardiac irritability and not from a conversion of sexuality into anxiety. Dammed-up sexual excitation must be regarded as the direct cause of anxiety in anxiety neurosis, as is nicotine in nicotine poisoning.

For the moment we shall keep in mind that anxiety may in one case be the result, and in another the cause, of vasomotor symptoms, as in fright, for instance. It is now our task to clarify as far as possible, or at least to define as problems, the relationships between vegetatively induced cardiac irritability and anxiety[1] on the one hand and sexuality and the vegetative nervous system on the other.

Research on angina pectoris has shown that irritation of the stimulus conductors that produce extrasystole, tachycardia, asystole, and so on, is accompanied by a more or less pronounced feeling of anxiety. Brissaud[2] feels that "inherent in every sensation relating to the heart, there exists characteristically a feeling of mortal danger." Rothberger states:

> The feeling of impending death [in angina pectoris] may not be viewed simply as a result of the pain; it is a specific sensation caused by the condition of the heart. If this were not true, the same feeling would also have to be present when severe pain occurs in peripheral regions due to other causes. Even when patients do not correctly localize the pain of angina pectoris, they still experience a type of pain altogether different from skin or muscle pain.

Lutembacher discovered that anxiety occurs even in mild cardiac dilatation. Braun characterizes the relationship between anxiety and heart symptoms as follows:

> In the healthy as well as the unhealthy heart, there is a specific (phylogenetic) response faculty that manifests

[1] In this we shall omit the anxiety occasionally experienced to the stomach instead of the heart.

[2] All the quotations in this paragraph are from Dimitrenko; "Das Problem der Angina Pectoris (Sammelreferat)," *Deutsche Medizinische Wochenschrift,* September, 1926.

itself in the form of anxiety sensation; indeed one might
say that a person cannot even think about his heart
without immediately feeling something akin to fear. In all
degrees of anxiety there occurs in the cardiac region a certain deep, frightening, constricting, stifling feeling which
increases with the degree of anxiety. It is a painful sensation, which at the peak of anxiety combines with the feeling of expiring.

Braun further calls it a feeling of the failure and "the
helplessness of the biological ego."

Concerning the causes of cardiac disorders that are not
bacterially or mechanically induced, the opinions of
physiologists diverge in detail but agree that the causes
must be sought in functional disturbances of the vegetative
nervous system, which, in turn, are caused by endocrine
disturbances. This view bears an important relationship to
the sex-economic theory, which also assumes disturbances
of the vegetative equilibrium to be the somatic basis of
neurosis.

The introduction of sexual stasis as one of the causes of a
disturbance of the vegetative equilibrium fills a gap in
physiology that, until now, has not even been recognized
as a problem. And yet every step forward in this area inevitably leads to the problem of sexuality.

Sexual Excitation and the Autonomic
Nervous System

Genital excitation and the anticipation of sexual
pleasure produce the same phenomena in the heart and
the vasomotor system as does anxiety. This most certainly
cannot be considered irrelevant for comprehension of the
relationship between anxiety and sexuality.

When we observe the vasomotor phenomena connected with the state of sexual excitation, we notice primarily the pounding of the heart and the physical sensation of warmth. There is also a sense of pleasurable and anxious anticipation intermingled, due to the fact that the pulse accelerates with the idea of impending danger just as it does with the expectation of sexual pleasure, producing the same specific sensation in the heart in both cases. It is as if the vivid imagining of a situation in which the vegetative nervous system plays an important role stimulates the vagus and sympathetic to test their functioning. Exact observation of this process—a process which can be triggered as often as one likes by fantasizing—shows that a very brief cardiac dilatation precedes acceleration of the pulse. Those kinesthetic sensations accompanying sexuality that are localized specifically in the cardiac area form the basis for numerous idioms such as "love lives in the heart," "to lose one's heart," "a generous heart" (applied to someone who is easily approachable), and so forth. In addition to this, the heart frequently signifies the genitals in symptoms and dreams. In a female patient the rhythmic throbbing of the excited clitoris was directly associated with the pounding of the heart. During sexual fantasies she pressed both hands to her heart in the same way she had pressed them to her clitoris prior to the repression of her masturbation desire.

We see further that the most important automatic functions in preparation for sexual acts are fulfilled by the vasovegetative system, for instance, vasodilatation in erection, secretion of Bartholin's glands* in women, and a general increased circulation of blood in the genitals. It may be said that sexual excitation due to pleasurable anticipation is initially identical with apprehensive anticipa-

* See footnote, page 25.

tion in that it involves the cardiac apparatus by way of vegetative innervation; but—to the extent that no inhibition is present—it subsequently shifts to the genital organ system, thus unburdening the cardiac system. The acceleration of the pulse during coitus is partly an expression of the excitation of the vegetative system; to a far greater degree it is the result of motor activity. The fact that emissions may occur in anxiety states clearly demonstrates the intimate connection between vegetatively induced excitation of the vascular system and that of the genital apparatus. Cases of masturbation during anxiety states also are pertinent here; the partial sexual discharge relieves the vegetative system of excitation, thereby diminishing the anxiety.

What now happens to the sexual excitation that at first was operative mainly in the realm of the vasovegetative system? In the beginning of the sexual act the excitation is concentrated more and more in the genitals. It is perceived as pleasure via sensory-nerve pathways and mounts to the climax. Thus, we may say that during the sexual act, excitation shifts increasingly from the vegetative to the sensory nervous system and finally, from the moment of climax, takes hold of the motor nervous system and the musculature. This transition involves unburdening of the vegetative nervous system and discharge of sexual excitation in the sensory-motor system. *The transition from the sensory to the motor system and the ebbing of excitation into the entire body is experienced as satisfaction.*

This description is supported by phenomenologically perceivable changes in the vasovegetative and sensory-motor systems before, during, and after coitus. It coincides essentially with Müller's[3] representation of the physiology of the orgasm. According to Müller, sexual ex-

[3] Müller, *Das vegetative Nervensystem* (Springer, 1920).

citation spreads from the smooth musculature of the genitals (spermatic cord and prostate) to the striated muscles, particularly the bulbo- and ischiocavernosi, lower pelvic muscles, and the extensors of the legs (demonstrated in experiments on a dog).

Müller further assumes that "when the orgasm occurs, the excitation spreads from the smooth musculature of the genitals to the rest of the vegetative nervous system as well." This, too, confirms our view that the orgasm constitutes a shift in the concentration of excitation in the vegetative system. One need only add that this occurs by way of the sensory-motor system. Accordingly, the following phases should be differentiated:

1. Accumulation of sexual energy in the vegetative system without tension.
2. Spontaneous or voluntary concentration of vegetative energy in the genitals (sexual tension and vasomotor phenomena).
3. Progressive transition to the sensory system (forepleasure; I and II in our sketch, Figure 5, p. 26).
4. Transition to the motor system (ascent to the climax and end pleasure; III and IV in Figure 5).
5. Flow back into the vegetative system; condition as in item 1 (V in sketch): The genitals and the sensory apparatus are relieved, the muscles relaxed.

We define orgasm as the processes described in items 4 and 5. As indicated, satisfaction is all the more complete (1) the more sexual energy is focused in the genitals and (2) the more completely, that is, the more undisturbedly, the excitation ebbs back into the vegetative system. We now comprehend better the basis of Freud's anxiety neuroses: If the transfer of sexual excitation to the sensory-motor nervous system and the genitals is prevented by some inhibition, the excitation is retained within the vasovegetative system and produces all the symptoms characteristic of vasomotor neurosis. This is most decidedly the case when there is a total lack of genital sensitivity due to psychic inhibitions and also when there is a frustration of excitation because the all-important transition from the sensory nervous system to the motor system does not occur.

In cases of coitus interruptus, I have encountered acute neurasthenia far more frequently than symptoms of anxiety neurosis. This is explained by the fact that although motor release occurs in coitus interruptus, the stimulatory process is grossly disturbed by the withdrawal. On the one hand, genital excitation of a predominantly sensory nature goes unreleased, resulting in typical neurasthenic symptoms; on the other hand, a greater or lesser amount of sexual excitation remains in the vegetative nervous system, partially affecting the cardiac system and partially producing disturbances of other autonomously innervated organs (for example, the intestines). Thus, there are transitions from the etiology of anxiety neurosis to neurasthenia that do not permit a clear separation of the two. In general, all one can say is that the closer the disturbance in the stimulatory process is to the point of motor release, the more prominently will acute neurasthenia emerge; the further the disturbance is from this point—that is, the less the vasovegetative nervous system is relieved—the more intense will be the symptoms of vasomotor neurosis and actual anxiety. We must expect a greater or lesser encumbering of the vegetative system in all neuroses.

In his first publication on anxiety neurosis Freud based his thinking on the fact that "anxiety neurosis is accompanied, in whole series of cases, by a most significant reduction of sexual libido, or psychic desire," and he concluded that *"the mechanism of anxiety neurosis . . . is to be sought in diversion of the somatic sexual excitation from the psychic, which process then causes the abnormal utilization of this excitement."* This "diversion from the *psychic"* can be brought about only through repression of perception of genital sensations. Somatically this means nothing other than prevention of the shift from the vegetative to the sensory-motor system. Apparently consciousness (Freud's Cs system) plays an important role in this. According to Freud, consciousness governs the access to motility. Becoming aware of a sexual impulse, that is, of a psychic portion of libido that expresses itself as a sexual desire, is a necessary prerequisite for sensitization of the sexual organs. This already constitutes a partial shift of excitation to the sensory system (pleasure sensation), and, indeed, we observe in analysis that anxiety increases as soon as even the perception of genital excitation is repressed, and abates when the perception is tolerated. If orgastic motor satisfaction does not occur, and if the sexual excitation does not become bound up in psychoneurotic symptoms, a renewed blocking of genital sensibility usually occurs, and the anxiety, including all the vasomotor phenomena, sets in once again. Of course this anxiety is no longer pure stasis anxiety in that it now also expresses the ego's "fear" of its own sexual needs. However, genital sensitivity decreases with the degree of nonperception (repression) of sexual excitation and, at the same time, feedback of excitation into the autonomic nervous system increases. These somatic processes are usually caused by psychic inhibitions, for example, fear of coitus.

Sexual satisfaction in the orgasm implies not only a release of nervous excitation but also a physiochemical revivification of other vegetative functions, which is more important for the organism as a whole. In this area a great deal of promising work awaits the efforts of physiological chemistry. I shall mention only the physical blossoming of the sexually satisfied woman as compared to the premature withering of the greatly ridiculed "old maid," who need not be any older than her happier sister. The same is also true of men. The so-called green-sickness* in postpubertal girls may likewise belong in this category. Further, it is striking that the anamneses of all women suffering from severe climacteric complaints reveal either an unhappy marriage and lasting frigidity, years of abstinence due to widowhood, or total genital abstinence due to never having been married. On the other hand, women who had happy marriages and did not have to suffer sexual stasis generally weather the climacteric without particular discomfort.

Finally, that biological rhythms are involved here, and neuroses are disturbances of these rhythms, is demonstrated by the fact that spring brings with it intensified sexual desire, higher suicide statistics, and an increase in neurotic disorders.

The Origin of Sexual-Stasis Neuroses

A Case of Vasomotor Neurosis

A twenty-six-year-old woman sought treatment for, among other symptoms, nightly spells of anxiety, pounding of the heart, trembling, hot flashes, and tearing of the eyes. She did not think her frigidity was pathological. On the contrary, sexual intercourse was a horror for her because she felt that it was animalistic and dirty; further-

*Chlorosis. [Trans.]

more, it caused her pain. The rest of her symptoms, which she did recognize as pathological, had appeared four years earlier; they were most severe in the evenings at about nine, when she sensed that her husband wanted to have intercourse with her. She admitted during the first interview that even when she was not suffering the symptoms, she acted as if she were, just to avoid her "marital duties."

The case could not be diagnosed as pure anxiety neurosis, in that her anxiety attacks, although lacking any definite content ("free-floating"), always began in the same way at approximately nine o'clock in the evening; in addition, the patient's character (masculine bearing, forced deep voice, matter-of-fact manner, etc.) seemed to imply a compulsion neurosis. Several months after the beginning of treatment it became apparent that her anxiety was characterized by indefinite anticipation anxiety as well ("as if something evil would happen").

The event that had caused the neurosis was an abortion her husband had forced her to have because he was in straitened financial circumstances. She had hated him ever since, whereas previously she had merely not thought very highly of him. The abortion had been a double shock; it meant the loss of the child and, more significant, a bloody genital intervention. The disappointment she felt at being denied the child was inconsistent with her masculine demeanor and her behavior during a second pregnancy that occurred in the course of her treatment. In keeping with her masculine bearing and compulsive personality, she had chosen a feminine man as her husband, a man whom she could dominate and torment. That he allowed her to do so was particularly infuriating to her and spurred her to torment him all the more. This contradictory behavior was explained by the role she assumed in her fantasies, that of tender wife loved by a strong and extremely rough husband. Analysis of this fantasy resulted in unusually rapid progress in recalling the experiences of early childhood.

In the third month of treatment, after the actual conflicts with her husband had been discussed in their essentials without remission of symptoms (all transference success was immediately unmasked as such and destroyed), she recalled numerous details of an anxiety hysteria that had occurred between the ages of three and seven. For example, she had been afraid of dark rooms and the idea of burglars.

Her parents' marriage had been very bad. The father was a drinker and a bully who tyrannized his wife and children. As a child the patient had at first been unable to understand why her father would be pleasant in the morning after having drunkenly abused her mother the night before. The father always came home very late, and the child fearfully anticipated the drunken scenes, knowing that they would be repeated every night. During further treatment she experienced severe anxiety sensations and accompanying vasomotor symptoms when she recalled the coitus scenes she had listened to for several years. They were the same symptoms she had experienced as a child and also during the last four years: anxiety, hot flashes, pounding of the heart, and urinary urgency. The analysis proceeded with great understanding on the patient's part, making possible a differentiation between two stages of listening to parental coitus. At first she had thought that something horrible was happening to her mother. Dreams indicated that she had awakened frightened the first time, and after that was unable to fall asleep at night because of fearful anticipation of what was to come. Gradually she grew accustomed to the nightly scenes and came to the conclusion that they could not be as bad as they seemed or her mother would not voluntarily get into her father's bed, nor could he be so amiable the next morning. She discovered the pleasurable aspects of the situation and from that time on masturbated during parental coitus. The same physical symptoms as had previously accompanied her anxiety now appeared in connection with sexual excitation. Nevertheless, masturbation always remained associated with anxiety, even after the impression created by the nightly scenes had been repressed. Finally, masturbation was also repressed, and there remained, as an unrecognizable vestige, the fear of the dark and of burglars. In addition to this, a fantasy formed that could likewise be traced to the bedroom scenes: her daydreams usually contained the thought of being "very, very rich." It came to my attention that these daydreams had completely replaced her fear at age seven. Since that time, and during puberty especially, she experienced a vague feeling of anxiety whenever she met a man she fancied. However, she always knew how to escape from dangerous situations and, curiously, fled into the "money fantasy." Occasionally she caught herself thinking she could become a prostitute to earn a lot of money. Along this line, she once dreamed she was walking through a dark, narrow street at night, with men she feared standing on every corner and in the recesses of the building walls. As a child she had been very interested in the women loitering about the streets. Once she had spoken to a prostitute and received money from her. She had wanted to bring this to her father to "put him in a good mood," because she knew money would calm him down. Thus, the money fantasy was a disguised incest fantasy apparently capable of binding her anxiety; if she had money she could put her father in a gentler frame of mind and win him for herself. It had not gone unnoticed that her mother achieved the same end by giving him money. This fantasy occurred without sexual excitation. On the other hand, she became genitally excited at the sight of a child or a dog being beaten. In the money and beating fantasies, anal-sadistic attitudes were expressed exactly as they were in her character, which we have termed compulsion-neurotic: she was totally frigid and sexually resistant, loved order, and was conscientious, masculine-tough, and cold.

After recollection of the bedroom scene, vasomotor symptoms appeared, at first connected with anxiety, particularly when details were discussed. Gradually, fear of genital excitation receded, while pounding of the heart, hot flashes, and the other vasomotor symptoms remained. The anxiety decreased in proportion to the increase in genital sensitivity. When she had pleasurable (though nonorgastic) intercourse for the first time with her husband, she conceived again. She had not used contraceptive measures in four years. Her present conception could be explained only by her having assumed the female sexual role. Prior to the sexual act in question, she had had several dreams containing symbolic expressions of the desire for a child. The transition to the female, motherly aspect also expressed itself clearly in her personality; she lost the pronounced hardness in her tone of voice, gait, and demeanor.

Despite this change in character and the remission of anxiety, treatment was continued. Masturbation anxiety, which expressed itself as a fear of having her genitalia touched, had not been discussed at all. The patient's fear of being injured during intercourse had also not become conscious, and penis desire, the basis of her masculine attitude, had hardly been mentioned. The success achieved was due solely to the mobilization of previously bound anxiety, which had included a quantum of sexual energy.

Due to advanced pregnancy, in the tenth month treatment was discontinued without its goals having been accomplished. The patient's husband had minor ejaculatio praecox, and although it did not disturb him, it did affect her liberated sexuality. In addition, the patient became involved in a new conflict which, thanks to treatment, she no longer attempted to solve through a neurotic reaction. Having been driven by her masculinity to marry a feminine man, she now yearned, in keeping with her new feminine attitude, for a strong husband to guide her. When I saw the patient again many months later, she was a happy mother but an unhappy wife. The anxiety had not returned, although she suffered from a slight gastric neurosis stemming from an unrelieved muscular hypertonicity. The source of this symptom could only be dammed-up sexual energy. Occasionally, sexual excitation was accompanied by hot flashes. The patient struggled against them in vain, unable to repress them. She intended to resume treatment in order to resolve the conflict with her husband.

She had only two alternatives. She could deny herself and accept her husband, seeking fulfillment in the performance of motherly duties and possible sublimation—and constantly risking a relapse, because sexual excitation can be effectively released only through orgasm. Or she could get a divorce and choose another husband. The conceivable solution of achieving satisfaction through masturbation promises little in the long run. In fact, it appears to be not without danger, due to the fantasies it involves.

I have discussed this patient's history at some length because the importance of physical sexual stasis for prognosis in a case of neurosis must be stressed. *In a symptom-free patient the propensity to relapse depends primarily on the amount of dammed-up sexual energy resulting from*

*the as-yet-unresolved inner inhibitions and external dif-
ficulties that hinder the establishment of an orderly sex
life.*

From the standpoint of theory this case can clarify some
connections between stasis-neurotic and purely psychoneurotic mechanisms. The following dynamics must be
differentiated:

1. The actual conflict with her husband employed
   the neurosis as a means to achieve neurotic goals
   (defense against coitus, torment of the husband).
   But this conflict itself was a result of mistaken
   identification caused by infantile experiences.

2. After being denied the child by her husband and
   experiencing the bloody genital intervention, the
   patient reactivated a situation that was primarily
   conditioned by the childhood bedroom experiences (nightly anxiety states). The reactivation
   of infantile sexual desire produced somatic sexual
   excitation that expressed itself in the same manner
   as it had in the past, through the stimulation of
   the vasomotor apparatus. Apart from the anxiety,
   the individual symptoms had no psychic significance. The anxiety signified the revived fear
   of the father's brutality, of sexual intercourse,
   and of her own incestuous desire. Due to her
   resistance, sexual excitability could not be evoked
   until she became ill. Sexual frigidity, a superstructure erected on a foundation of genital anxiety
   and serving as a protection from sexual stimuli,
   crumbled only under the strong impact of revived
   infantile fantasies.

3. However, genital anxiety prevented genital sensitivity, and excitation could thus become man-

ifest only as stasis anxiety. It follows that the vasomotor symptoms, tremors, and vertigo, etc. were the expression of sexual excitation that was denied access to the genitals. Thus the psychic need for love, which in this context may be described as a yearning for the father, was augmented by physical excitation that intensified the anxiety. This, in turn, caused a constant rekindling of the vasomotor neurosis, which started the cycle over again. Hence, the genital anxiety and character-rooted rejection of sex were the indirect psychic causes of the stasis anxiety.

Physical sexual stasis may be brought about in two ways. In one, a slight psychic inhibition prevents satisfaction but does not diminish excitation. This unresolved sexual excitation causes generalized restlessness, irritability, and ill humor, as well as physical symptoms, and becomes a source of ever increasing discomfort. Genital stimulation becomes unpleasurable, occasionally even painful, and is finally avoided. At this point vasomotor symptoms and anxiety become prominent. Disturbance of the sexual equilibrium is then brought to bear secondarily on the ever-present latent psychic conflicts.

In the other course of physical sexual stasis a strong character-rooted inhibition, such as the one seen in the last case, does not even allow excitation to occur, so vegetative tensions remain slight at first and find release in the numerous opportunities offered by daily life. Then, due to a more or less important actual cause—which, however, is always associated with early conflicts and becomes pathogenic for this reason—infantile conflicts are reactivated as sexual fantasies. Through this reactivation, what was originally a slight sexual stasis is now endowed with pathogenic force. Secondarily, the sexual stasis aggravates the psychic conflict and becomes the real source of energy for the symptoms, which, as previously stressed, emerge only after a certain interval occupied with the conscious or unconscious fantasy activity that was first responsible for creating the stasis.

In advanced neurotic states it is only with great difficulty that we are able to differentiate between the psychic and somatic causal elements of sexual stasis. The difference that exists between stasis neurosis and psychoneurosis in their initial stages is decisive. In stasis neurosis there is first a damming-up of vegetative energy, which, if it continues over a period of time, causes regression and psychic stasis (unfulfilled yearning). In psychoneurosis, actual situations, such as disappointment in the love object or narcissistic injury, stimulate early desires and infantile fantasies, and these, secondarily, cause the pathogenic damming-up of sexual energy. However, we must stress the fact that this type of flight into childhood, or rather into the illness, is more apt to occur, and is more readily caused by trivial incidents, the less the sexual attachment to the love partner and the less real sexual satisfaction exists.

Thus, no stasis neurosis can emerge without psychic inhibitions or disturbances of the genital function, nor can a psychoneurosis emerge without a damming-up of sexual energy. Furthermore, the longer a stasis neurosis lasts, the greater will be the neurotic superstructure.

The psychoneurotic part of a neurosis corresponds to its historical etiology (Oedipus complex); the stasis-neurotic portion corresponds to the *actual* disturbance of the vegetative equilibrium. Figure 9 illustrates the typical relationships: (1) The Oedipus complex provides the basic material (content, fantasies), and the sexual stasis, the

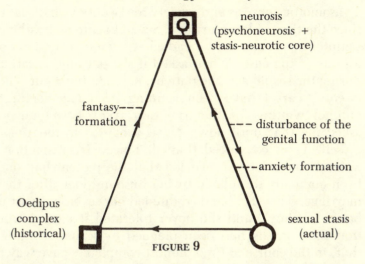

FIGURE 9

energy, for the creation of the neurosis. (2) Sexual stasis transforms the Oedipus complex from an historical fact into a topical one; this then causes the acute sexual stasis to become chronic by inhibiting the genital function.

Thus the ring of the two etiologies closes to form a continuous cycle: fantasy, disturbance of the genital function, sexual stasis, anxiety; fantasy, disturbance of the genital function, etc. For example, a recently married man complained of severe spells of anxiety, with pounding of the heart, tremors, and sudden sweats—symptoms that had first appeared a year earlier. When I inquired about his sexual life, he reported that for a year prior to the emergence of the anxiety neurosis, he had practiced coitus interruptus to prevent a second unwanted pregnancy. Somewhat later the anxiety assumed a definite content; he was frequently awakened by dreams in which he was being pursued, dreams similar to those he had experienced only during his childhood.

A forty-year-old female patient had been suffering from

a vasomotor neurosis and anxiety for twenty years, that is, since the time of her marriage. Several acute neurasthenic symptoms (backaches, headaches) were complicating aspects of the case. When asked if she felt any sensations during the sexual act, the patient, in tears, burst out, "For twenty years I have been running from one doctor to another waiting for that question. Why hasn't anyone asked me that until now? I was ashamed to mention it myself. I am convinced that all I need is satisfaction." Several conversations revealed that the patient had once been manually stimulated by her husband soon after their marriage. This "act" had frightened her severely (masturbation anxiety), and she never tolerated it again. From that time on she had been plagued by sexual excitation that, in the course of time, almost completely gave way to the neurotic symptoms or occurred alternately with them. My attempt to remove her psychic inhibition through suggestion was temporarily successful, and the patient experienced her first orgasm through stimulation of the clitoris. The symptoms vanished at once. A second, unsuccessful attempt merely left the patient in a state of excitation whereupon the symptoms reappeared with the same intensity. Psychic inhibition, presumably a severe masturbation guilt, had yielded momentarily to a strong transference but could have been permanently eliminated only by means of a thorough character analysis.

Here any direct effect of suggestion must be ruled out. Character-analytic treatment offers repeated evidence of the symptomatic relief afforded by genital orgasm. This connection first occurred to me during the analysis of a compulsion-neurotic character suffering from inability to work, compulsive brooding, and sexual timidity. After approximately eight months of treatment, the patient's fixation on his mother and sister (fixation on the latter was more actual) had abated to the extent that he engaged in intercourse for the first time, with full satisfaction in every respect. His complaints vanished overnight; he reported having a "clear head" and feeling "like a newborn babe." Over the course of eight days the symptoms gradually returned, only to disappear again following a second coition. This pattern was repeated for six consecutive weeks.

Hysteria with Hypochondriacal Anxiety

A thirty-two-year-old married woman came to me because of an agonizing fear that she and her eight-year-old son might die of tuberculosis. She had consulted a physician three years before because the child had not been looking well. The examination had revealed no pathological condition, and the doctor had merely pointed out the danger of inflammation of the apices of the lungs. She gave it no further thought until the boy fell ill with diphtheria two years later. She then began to worry in a compulsively hypochondriacal fashion, although it did not assume the character of anxiety. However, when the boy recovered, her worry did not cease; on the contrary, it intensified, despite the physician's repeated assurances that there was nothing wrong. Concern for the child now began to cause insomnia, and this rendered her incapable of work. Crying spells and acute anxiety states appeared; she continually thought, "But what if my child were to die!"

The first weeks of treatment provided clear insight into the real cause of her illness. First, she remembered that while the boy was lying ill in bed, she had been tormented by the fear that her thirteen-year-old daughter might induce him to masturbate. Shortly before, she had seen her daughter masturbating but had not been particularly concerned. Some time later the patient experienced severe disappointment in her husband with whom, until then, she had had a reasonably good marriage; she had seen him flirt with, and kiss, a young girl. The patient was furiously jealous. (She stated that she was so faithful to her husband that her entire body trembled in fear if another man so much as looked at her.) After the incident, she experienced an irresistible urge to masturbate, and on the following night she dreamed of having intercourse *a tergo* with her father, who had died eight years before. She had never experienced such intense pleasure sensations during intercourse with her husband as those she had in the dream. From then on, the hypochondriacal concern intensified and assumed the character of anxiety.

During puberty she herself had masturbated excessively until she read about the supposed dangers of masturbation. She believed, for example, that it could cause syphilis. After she met her husband she masturbated very rarely, ceasing altogether once she engaged in regular sexual intercourse. She was vaginally hypesthetic, suffered frequently from vaginismus, and was inhibited in every respect. For years sexual relations with her husband had consisted of penile thrusting against the vulva, which only partially satisfied her.

If we systematically examine the causes of her illness, we see that anxiety, the last and most severe symptom, arose only after the dream of coitus with her father in which she experienced pleasurable genital sensations. Even long before this, her psychic balance was unstable; she had been struggling with a desire to masturbate, had been vaginally hypesthetic to a high degree, and orgastically impotent. After the episode between her husband and the girl, she fled into fantasies, and masturbation desires dominated once again. At the time her son fell ill, repression was already weak. The content for the impending anxiety was then supplied by the physician's mention of tuberculosis—the disease that had claimed her father's life. The energy was derived from fear of masturbation, which had been rekindled by her daughter's masturbation, although it did not emerge immediately as affective anxiety. Resistance against masturbation assumed an anxious quality only after she experienced intense sexual excitation in the dream. In keeping with her old attitudes, she saw death or ruination as the inevitable consequence of masturbation. Masturbation desire, as well as fear of punishment, was projected onto the boy. There were special reasons for this, as illustrated by the following dream:

> There was a green meadow; suddenly I saw my boy sitting on a so-called field railway. He was holding the steering wheel in his hand like a driver, going forward and backward. When I called him and rushed to stop him, he drove backward; if I rushed back toward him, he drove forward. Suddenly I caught sight of my dead sister and wanted to punish her instead of the boy, but she was so small that she hardly needed to bend over in order to duck under one of the axles. I just managed to catch her by the hand and slapped her face several times with my left hand. In doing so, I had a peculiar feeling, as if my hand had to fit her face perfectly. Each time it was very difficult to free my hand from her cheek and strike again.

The patient immediately grasped the significance of the steering wheel and the "back and forth" in the dream. Since she had played "doctor" with other children for years during childhood and puberty, she was forced to admit that she herself had harbored the desire to seduce her son; but the resistance against this desire became conscious only in her concern that her daughter might attempt to seduce him. This realization should have been sufficient. Why, then, was her anxiety over the consequences of her own masturbation shifted to the boy? Furthermore, why had the anxiety not erupted when she saw her daughter masturbating?

Among her compulsive fears ran one recurrent idea, namely, that her boy would not live to reach the age of eighteen. She recalled that her elderly mother and eighteen-year-old brother had slept together in the marriage bed. This was a memory she could not come to terms with. She herself had slept with her own son until she started treatment. Their sleeping position was indicative enough: the boy was made to lie with his back to her, her hand covering his genitalia. She always washed and bathed him herself, but avoided touching his genitalia. With the intensification of repression, this developed into a pronounced fear of contact.

In addition, the boy had assumed the significance of a penis in her unconscious fantasies; more correctly stated, she transferred to him all the interest she had been forced to withdraw from her clitoris. This explained the desire she had had at his birth that he remain small, that is, like a phallus. Thus, at the deepest level, loss of the boy signified loss of her own penis.

The clearest indication of the patient's desire for a penis was that she preferred to urinate standing over the toilet. She never forgot how greatly she had envied little boys for their ability to direct the stream of their urine. Her unconscious wish was that treatment would help her obtain a penis; her hope of being cured signified only this. After two months her symptoms vanished, but treatment was continued nonetheless, because she could not get over the idea that she was still unwell. When, as a result of positive transference, her fear of a relapse grew very strong, she recalled that she had once told her husband that he could go to the tavern, providing he left her his penis.

There is a very characteristic dream from this phase of treatment. To clarify it I must explain that, just as "boy" represented "penis" to her, "little, or dead, sister" implied "castrated genital."

> I had to climb a mountain with a gazebo at the top. All at once my little sister [her genital] was with me, and leaves lay piled up in front of the summerhouse.* Two thick tree trunks [penis] lay horizontally across everything. My sister was in a hurry and busily doing something [clitoral masturbation]. Suddenly everything began to slide [orgasm: *cf.* her dream in the chapter on orgasm disturbances], and I saw my sister lying at the bottom of the hill, her body half covered by the trunks [rape fantasies]. Then I rushed to you and asked you to help my sister [her genital] and examine her [playing "doctor"–masturbation], but you always said "No" [denial in treatment], and then I thought, "Oh, well! You don't want to, it's all due to the treatment, because I would not be able to speak if I knew you had examined my sister [silence always indicated a concealment of sexual desires and excitation]. Then I was very angry at you.

This dream occurred shortly after I had announced the termination of her treatment. Following this announcement, the patient was tormented by acute urinary urgency for the remainder of the session.

Although the penis fantasy did have its own pathogenic power, it was augmented by the connection with masturbation and genital anxiety. When her husband wanted to go to the tavern, the patient asked him to leave his penis

*The literal translation is "house of pleasure"; Reich underlines the word in German. [Trans.]

with her. In addition, she identified with her father following the inevitable disappointment in her love life. She had lost her father to tuberculosis and feared she herself would die of this disease. Once, during puberty, her father had caught her masturbating. Although he did not scold her, she knew that he was angry. From then on, her inclination toward masculine achievements and competition with boys intensified. Nevertheless, she remained essentially feminine. It became evident that the patient's desire for a penis and hypochondriacal apprehensiveness, which was unmasked as genital anxiety, always grew more severe when she was disappointed or rejected or when polygamous desires became active, resulting in fear of other men. This was manifested first as a generalized fear of me, and later as a fear of being raped.

At this time her infantile relationship to her father was also clarified. Among other things, the fact that she had given birth to her own daughter at the same time that her mother bore her youngest girl was an important contributing factor. Both children were given the same name. The patient took care of both and fantasized having two children, both begotten by her father. The following is a dream from this period:

My father was lying in my husband's bed, just the way my husband does. I was crying terribly and told him how badly my sister [her genital] had behaved [guilt feelings due to masturbation and the incest fantasy]. While I was relating this and sobbing, I walked into the kitchen, pulled a curtain across the window, and placed dark paper over it [she was in the habit of doing this before sexual intercourse with her husband].

A further highly significant root of her fear for the boy was a strongly repressed death wish, which likewise originated in her love of her father. At the time of her son's birth the father lay on his deathbed, and in her despair she wondered if he would live were the child to die in his stead. In one dream, she was gathering mushrooms in the woods when her father suddenly appeared and the boy "faded into the shadows." In another she dreamed as follows:

> I cut off both my boy's feet and ate them. I was supposed to cut off another piece of him, but he was still alive, so I said to my husband, "First I will take off his head." During all this my husband was trying to persuade me to take the little boy to the hospital. Then it occurred to me that I had already shed a great many tears for the boy, and that I could not imagine how he was ever to reach the age of twenty, now that I had made him a cripple. At that I was overcome by a yearning to make amends for all I had done. I was filled with the desire to heal him, but without taking him to a doctor, because he would know what I had done.

Let us summarize the determinants of the hypochondriacal anxiety:

1. "I have been disappointed by my husband and shall return to my father, who will satisfy me." [Incest dream–masturbation wish.]
2. "I am afraid of losing my son [a father substitute] to tuberculosis as well."
3. "I wish my child would die so that my father would return."
4. "I would like to induce my boy to masturbate but fear he will die of the results." [Orgasm–genital anxiety.]
5. "I would like to dismember my son and possess his penis."

6. "My boy is my penis; I would like to masturbate with him [penis] but fear I will lose him [it] for this [as punishment]."

While the patient was suppressing her genital impulses and genital anxiety was causing her hypochondriacal anxiety, physical excitation, which could not be released genitally, was released instead in the form of an unyielding symptom. Large urticarial wheals, which she called "blisters," appeared on her left arm and cheek. The patient noticed that the "blisters" appeared only on the left (I was sitting on her left). On one of the following days, just as she was discussing her shyness about being seen by men while in her bathing suit, very itchy "blisters" appeared on her legs above the garters. She then remembered that when she was approximately ten, a boy had reached under her dress. The thought of a man looking at her with desire or touching her had caused wheals for some time. She then remarked spontaneously that nothing in the world could make her undress in my presence. When she went swimming, she was ashamed of her naked arms and legs and especially of her breasts, which she felt were too small. The urticaria occurred in all situations in which women usually blush.

When the wheals appeared during puberty, she blamed them on her previous excessive masturbation. Many years later, after she was married, itching "blisters" appeared whenever she suffered intensely from her inability to achieve satisfaction. The following facts prove that this was an instance in which excitation, blocked from release through the genitals, emerged on the skin. For a long while the patient resisted the explanation that she had not given up masturbation permanently, as she claimed, but had merely repressed the desire for it. After several

months, during which she came to accept this explanation, she confessed that at the time of her most intense
resistance to it, urticarial wheals had appeared on the
labia majora, causing her to scratch them continually. She
had done this without realizing that the scratching con-
stituted full-fledged masturbation. Just as she had been
frightened by genital excitation prior to her illness, she
later feared the "blisters," which she took to be a great
misfortune and a symptom of her illness.

Urticaria also occurred when the patient felt the need to
urinate during a session and was ashamed to say that she
had to use the toilet. The blisters also appeared when she
splashed herself with water or stepped into a bath. During
childhood she had passed through a stage of enuresis. For
many years she had had a recurrent dream in which someone surprised her while she was washing the laundry. This
dream remained obscure until it occurred to her that during puberty she had employed the rhythmical washing
motion to rub her genitalia on the edge of the tub. When
she began to resist masturbation, very itchy urticarial
wheals appeared over her whole body whenever she did
the laundry. Later she recalled that the first "blisters"
had appeared on the back of the thighs when she was eight
years old; she was working in the garden with her father,
who was a gardener. The patient was vehemently opposed
to, and slightly afraid of, coitus from behind. In dreams,
however, she had intercourse with her father in this very
position. As a small child she had eagerly observed the
mating of animals and had decided that her parents practiced the same mode of coitus. In her marital relationship
she often felt a strong desire for coitus from behind and
reacted to this desire with spells of anxiety. Thus, each
localization of the "blisters" corresponded to the area
associated with any particular fantasy (labia, to masturba-

tion; gluteal region, to coitus from behind; thighs, to the fantasy that someone was reaching underneath her dress).

The "blisters" signified shame over sexual cravings. The energy that these ideas employed to produce the symptoms was physical genital excitation (energy source of the symptom), the same energy that at other times caused irritation of the vegetative system or anxiety. Particularly striking was the regularity with which anxiety subsided as soon as urticaria occurred and increased when the symptom, which she dreaded with good reason, disappeared. She seemed to have grasped intuitively that the urticaria was to be condemned as much as masturbation. However, even during the period of reduced anxiety, genital anxiety was still present. It was genital anxiety that was, after all, primarily responsible for excitation being diverted from the genitals to the skin.

CHAPTER FIVE

Forms
of Genital
Impotence

Are Sexual Disorders Neurotic Symptoms?
What Is a Neurotic Symptom?

In anxiety neurosis and anxiety hysteria, sexual excitation has but one fate: it is resisted and barred from genital release. Sexual energy as such survives, however. Stasis anxiety, which may now emerge as fear of catastrophe, hypochondria, or overt anxiety, is not a symptom in Freud's sense. His definition of the neurotic symptom stresses the fact that it represents a new formation, a compromise arising from the conflict between a repressed drive and a repressing moral agency; in other words, it is a pathological resolution of the conflict. This is not true for stasis anxiety, which simply appears in place of the sexual affect, nor for the fear of sexual activity. As long as anxiety dominates the neurosis, no resolution of the conflict has been found. Resolution can be said to have occurred only when circumscribed conversion-hysterical or compulsion-neurotic symptoms appear and take over from, or at least diminish, the anxiety. This implies the "binding of

109

neurotic anxiety" (Freud) as is convincingly demonstrated in almost every case in which symptoms are eliminated in analysis, for if the corresponding drive force does not achieve satisfaction or sublimation immediately, anxiety reappears. For this reason compulsion neurotics become anxious when they suppress their compulsive behavior. If hysterical vomiting disappears due to suggestion, it is replaced by anxiety states or anxiety dreams, which usually contain rape fantasies. Anxiety also occurs when impulsive characters suppress their sadistic impulses or when homosexuals stop masturbating. The anxiety thus liberated always has the character both of drive resistance and the affect associated with stasis anxiety.

Hence, anxiety replaces inhibited sexual excitation and can, in turn, be replaced by other symptoms. In all cases a *plus* function in one area of psychic activity is created that corresponds to a *minus* function in another area. Consequently, we must differentiate between the two functions:

1. Plus functions comprise neurotic symptoms, in the Freudian sense, and also anxiety. They disturb psychic equilibrium by absorbing psychic energy, are subjectively torturous, socially distressing, and biologically purposeless.

2. Minus (inhibited or deficient) functions comprise those neurotic symptoms that represent not compromise formations but simply deficiencies in normal functioning caused by the drawing-off of energy into the inappropriate plus function. The compulsive brooder simultaneously complains of his brooding and an inability to keep his mind on his work; the claustrophobic at some crucial point in social relationships or in the love function experiences a deficiency of energy because of that expended by his phobia; an individual who feels

inferior actually does achieve less because he expends in daydreams of sex and success the energy that could easily remove his inferiority feelings.

The disorders of the genital function are evident in all the inhibitions of function. They are not neurotic symptoms in the strict sense, since they do not correspond to disguised gratification of sexual drive impulses. On the contrary, they are the precipitating factor in the disguised, unconscious attempts to discharge energy in a symptom.

Thus our objective in this section will be to show what other outlets are available to blocked sexual excitation when it does not emerge as an anxiety affect. I shall limit myself to a brief description of hysterical and compulsive symptoms and the genital asthenia seen in chronic neurasthenics.

Hysterical Impotence

Since Freud, conversion has been defined as the process by which "amounts of psychic affect are directed toward abnormal organ innervation." In addition, the hysterical "organ language" likewise expresses psychic desires. However, our research compels us to conclude that a "leap from the psychic to the somatic" can by no means be taken for granted, since (1) vegetative sexual excitation is, as we have found, functionally identical with the psychic idea, and (2) a psychic desire, occurring with only the minutest quantities of vegetative excitation concentrated in the correlative organ, can center, for either a short period of time or permanently, great quantities of excitation in the erogenous zone involved.

The healthy person develops neither hypochondria nor

conversion symptoms because he has no dammed-up sexual energy. In reality there can be no conversion hysteria without a rather strong admixture of anxiety hysteria because hysterical individuals, with their extreme emphasis upon the genitals, do not succeed in releasing the full measure of genital excitation. The unbound remainder emerges as stasis anxiety. In the conversion symptom, on the other hand, the satisfying character of the symptom outweighs the resistance. This may be seen, for example, in the urticaria of the female patient described in the preceding chapter, or in *arc de cercle*. Naturally, conversion symptoms provide merely substitute satisfaction, that is, inadequate motor release; there is no question of satisfaction in the sense of sexual sensations, because the generation of pleasure sensations is dependent on willingness to perceive and enjoy them. Sexual energy, which ordinarily causes stimulation of the genitals, is being used for the pathological excitation of other organs, the selection of which is determined by the particular aim that the energy serves, an aim banned from consciousness just as the genital sensation itself is. Hysterical "organ language" is thus primarily the expression of genital longings and desires.

Although the conversion process may occur in any organ, "preference" is usually given to those especially well suited to express genital desires because of their particular erogenous character, their value as genital symbols (body orifices and protrusions), or their associative relationship to genital functioning (e.g., stomach—pregnancy).

What psychoanalysts once described as "accumulation of libido at the point of conversion or of hypochondriacal sensation" is not a material accumulation; it is a concentration of vegetative (electrical) excitation at that point because of an interference with the metabolism of vegetative energy.

The fact that very few conversion processes occur in the genitals themselves is characteristic of the general neurotic tendency to exclude the genitals from conscious thought. What we do find in the genital area is all forms of hysterical impotence that are merely functional inhibitions and not symptoms in the strict sense. Amenorrhea and sterility are functional inhibitions only, although occasionally amenorrhea may also correspond to a pregnancy fantasy. During analysis of some hysterical women who have severely repressed their masturbation desires, eczema appears on the genitalia before these desires become conscious. In such cases it is difficult to decide whether the eczema is due to a conversion process or merely caused by masturbation during sleep; many aspects of its appearance and disappearance argue for the former possibility. The eczema provides an excuse to scratch the genitalia without the patient having to become aware of the real meaning of her actions. Indeed, in one case a patient developed genital eczema whenever she refrained from acting on her conscious masturbation desires, even during the daytime.

As an example of psychogenic amenorrhea involving a pregnancy fantasy, I shall cite the case of a nineteen-year-old patient who missed her period for nine months following the death of her mother. Immediately after the funeral the patient had gone on a trip with her father and had forgotten to pack sanitary napkins, a clear indication of her unconscious intent not to menstruate, that is, to bear a child.

Nevertheless, the true domains of the conversion process lie outside the genital region, in the oral and anal zones as well as the skin. The oral zone comprises not only the oral cavity but, from a functional standpoint, also the larynx, pharynx, stomach, bronchia, nose, and additionally, the skin of the face, cranium, and the breasts. The corresponding conversion symptoms are hysterical vomiting (a weaker form may be seen in disgust toward food in general or only toward certain foods), globus hystericus, functional pylorospasm, nervous bronchial asthma, mutism and hysterical aphonia, the blushing of erythrophobia, as well as certain forms of headache.

In the anal region the most typical symptoms are hysterical obstipation and (more rarely) diarrhea as an expression of a deflection of a parasympathetic sexual excitation. I have already discussed in detail the differences in psychic content between these manifestations and the intestinal symptoms of chronic neurasthenia in my paper "Die chronische hypochondrische Neurasthenie"* (*Internationale Zeitschrift für Psychoanalyse*, 1926).

In the case of the skin and its adjunctive organs, psychogenic urticaria and pathological blushing are predominantly conversion symptoms. I would remind the reader of the psychic mechanisms that caused urticaria in the female patient suffering from hypochondriacal anxiety and cite one further example: A twenty-six-year-old man was receiving treatment for intense blushing and anxiety. As is always the case in erythrophobia, sexual excitation, displaced to the face, played a central role. One day the patient did not appear for treatment. (On the preceding day I had touched on the topic of anxiety concerning his penis.) The next day he related the following: he had been ready to leave his apartment for his session, when an enormous, itching, urticarial swelling appeared on his upper lip. Soon thereafter, clearly defined, red-margined

---

* "Chronic, hypochondriacal neurasthenia." [Trans.]

urticarial blisters appeared on the backs of his hands, and his penis became swollen. As he described it, it grew "to a gigantic size and became spongy and soft." Anticipating that that day's session would lead to a discussion of masturbation and penis anxiety, he had dreaded the idea of going to it. Anxiety over further discussion of his impotence had brought on an as-yet-physiologically-incomprehensible disturbance of vegetative genital excitation that, in actuality, confirmed his feeling of ruined potency.

Other dermatological manifestations, primarily those which are also seen in anxiety neurosis, such as perspiring, blanching, blushing, and so on, may have a conversion-hysterical character, although not necessarily. In other words, such symptoms do not always contain unconscious ideas.

Within the muscle system, well-known conversion symptoms are psychogenic tic, a masturbation equivalent (*cf.* Stekel, Ferenczi, Reich, Deutsch, Kovács); astasia and abasia, about which little is known as yet; and *arc de cercle*, which represents coitus itself.

The analysis of conversion symptoms localized in the anal and oral zones demonstrates that the mouth, throat, trachea, intestines, feces, and so forth, assume in the unconscious the significance of the genitals or their functions (Freud, Ferenczi, Abraham). However, the selection of the organ is determined by its inherent erogeneity which attracts to itself the excitation barred from the genitals. In the treatment of potency disturbances it is most important to crystallize out the genital excitability. For despite the deflection of vegetative excitation from the genitals, the genital desire has not been relinquished.

Inhibitions of the genital function in both anxiety hysteria and conversion hysteria are caused by a displacement of sexual excitation from the genitals as described above. The dynamic relationship of such inhibitions to hysterical symptoms accounts for the fact that the various hysterical inhibitions of genitality maintain a certain form; that is, they are characterized by a clearly recognizable and, in contrast to compulsion neurosis, immediate fear of genital injury (including castration anxiety). The fear of "bursting" or "exploding" as a result of strong genital excitation is never absent.[1]

Neurotic abstinence, resulting from conscious or easily recognizable unconscious sexual anxiety, is the typical form of hysterical impotence in both sexes.[2] Very frequently, patients first recognize their neurosis, or the illness develops to its full extent, when the initial attempt at coition is either unsuccessful or very disappointing. The former is more frequent in men, the latter, in women. In girls, any attempt to find a sexual partner is usually prevented by moral inhibitions, which join with inner inhibitions caused by infantile denial. Thus they fall ill, either during or after puberty, or they tolerate the prohibitions and later, when they marry and must give up abstinence, become neurotic because of their incapacity.

Men usually cite fear of impotence as the motive for abstinence. Girls from a milieu oppressed by strong compulsive morality are rarely aware of their sexual timidity, let alone its connection with neurosis. Occasionally they answer inquiries regarding their sexual lives by saying that

[1] The basic feature of all genital disorders is that, as a result of an as-yet-not-fully-understood physiological process rooted in psychosexual anxiety, the direction of the charge "toward the genitals" is reversed "away from the genitals." Thus, the penis shrinks when it should become engorged and the vagina becomes dry instead of moist.

[2] Ideologically approved abstinence of long duration must be viewed as a special form of impotence, because experience shows that when individuals decide to have intercourse after a long period of abstinence, genital disorders sooner or later emerge.

they are suffering from an unhappy love affair or that their lover is so "animalistic" and demands "indecencies." "However," they continue, "that has nothing to do with my illness." Later we shall demonstrate the close relationship between male impotence and sexual timidity in women.

It is not always easy to recognize abstinence as neurotic. One hears the most credible as well as the most improbable rationalizations for abstinence. Men, for example, claim that they do not engage in sexual intercourse because of a lack of opportunity or money or because vocational and other concerns are so demanding that they do not have time to think of "such matters"; sometimes ethical and religious motives also provide a pretext. One of the most frequent neurotic rationalizations for abstinence is the fear of venereal disease. Other patients justify their abstinence by saying they cannot afford to have children. Proof that this is indeed mere rationalization is provided by the fact that people who have no knowledge of other contraceptive measures usually practice coitus interruptus.

The continued abstinence of young widows is always neurotic; they are unable to accept a new partner either because of strong feelings of guilt toward their deceased husband or because of an exaggerated fixation on him. The end of mourning, the function of which is to make possible the overcoming of loss, is a sign of psychic health.

Thus far we have considered abstinence only in regard to sexual intercourse. Total abstinence, which excludes every form of direct sexual satisfaction, is very rarely encountered. Experience gained in treating patients who think they are totally abstinent shows that extreme skepticism is necessary in such cases. Patients tend either to withhold information about autoerotic satisfaction completely or to be totally unaware of it if it is achieved in a more or less disguised form. All forms of "masked" genital and extragenital masturbation, as well as "masturbation equivalents" (Ferenczi), belong to this group.

Forms of Hysterical Impotence in Men

1. Facultative or partial erective impotence: the loss of, or the inability to have, an erection before coition. Spontaneous erective capability is usually not disturbed during masturbation or in masturbation fantasies.
2. The mild form of premature ejaculation (ejaculatio praecox of the genital phase). Whether the erection is full or partial, ejaculation occurs just before or shortly after the beginning of the act due to anxiety.
3. Severe reduction of orgastic potency in all instances.

Forms of Hysterical Impotence in Women

1. Disturbance of vaginal sensation.
2. Total orgastic impotence in all instances.

Hysterical, as opposed to compulsion-neurotic, women are never frigid, that is, never completely unexcitable. On the contrary, with the exception of the genitals, they are sexually oversensitive. Hysterical reactions (ovarian pain, sensitivity of the mammae, etc.) show no psychic meaning but rather are direct expressions of displaced genital excitation. In some female hysterics the clitoris is so easily excited that the slightest stimulation produces orgasmlike sensations. This fact usually deceives both physician and patient in regard to recognizing orgastic impotence. Obviously, this short-circuited excitation no more has the economic value of a normal orgasm than does the excitation involved in premature ejaculation. During intercourse such women are usually anxious and vaginally insensitive.

Impotence in the Compulsion Neurotic

It would exceed the limits of this work to attempt to demonstrate the influence of sexual stasis and stasis anxiety on the formation of the compulsive character. All the character traits of compulsion neurotics prove to be defense mechanisms, not only against satisfaction (as in hysteria) but also against anxiety itself, which derives its strength from dammed-up sexual energy. Compulsive symptoms "bind" (Freud) neurotic anxiety; stasis anxiety appears immediately if compulsive actions are consciously suppressed. Thus, compulsive symptoms, like hysterical symptoms, are plus functions, although they are active primarily in cognitive areas. They derive their cathexis from dammed-up sexual energy, as do hysterical symptoms. Here the object is merely to prove that compulsion neurotics actually have dammed-up sexuality at their disposal and to establish the differences between compulsive and hysterical impotence.

Unlike hysterics, the compulsive character has not maintained the genital conflict but has avoided it by regression to the anal-sadistic phase of sexual development (Freud). He has replaced genital substitute satisfaction with anal substitute satisfaction and even protected himself against these through vigorous anal reaction-formations (exaggerated orderliness and cleanliness, ceremonials, etc.). Sadism, however, becomes, among other things, a means of warding off "genital danger."

An excerpt from the analysis of a compulsion neurotic suffering chronic depression may serve to illustrate the above:

A thirty-two-year-old woman, a virgin, with stern, masculine features and brusque, unfeminine mannerisms and appearance, came to me for relief from recent anxiety states. She did not regard her inability to experience pleasure as pathological. Although she suffered greatly because of it, she bore it as her "fate." Recently she had made the acquaintance of a young man whom she suddenly began to hate vehemently, at first without knowing why. Later she rationalized the hate with various far-fetched motives. She had noticed that she hated him most when he was kind and friendly to her. Gradually she began to experience intense anxiety every time she saw him. To this she reacted with intensified hate and sadistic fantasies. It soon became clear that she had fallen in love with the man without being willing to recognize this and that she was attempting to weaken her love by forced hatred. Hate and anxiety intensified each other in a vicious circle, dominating her alternately until severe depression finally set in. During her states of depression she was compelled to eat a great deal. In one such phase she dreamed that she was ravenously consuming frankfurters. She consciously fantasized trampling the man to a pulp and squashing his penis with the heel of her shoe. When she recognized the nature of her anxiety, both it and the sadistic fantasies ceased. However, she transferred her love to me and began to resist it in the same manner, namely, by hating me and overeating. No anxiety occurred. Finally she terminated the treatment saying that she had achieved her goal; she was no longer in love with the man, had nothing left to fear, and therefore had no further need for treatment. She refused to accept my explanation that she was running away.[3]

The patient's infatuation corresponded to a hysteriform surge of sexuality toward genital drive goals and a real partner. In rejecting it, she developed anxiety—a product of stasis and resistance anxiety. The forced hate and sadistic fantasies that alternated with the anxiety represented flight into compulsion neurosis with aggressive defense against the man she felt as a threat (not against the drive itself). This aggressive defense against genital danger appeared in the form of oral destruction of the dangerous penis. The states of depression corresponded to this unconscious process. Flight from genital demands, with aggressive resistance to the object arousing them, is a specific compulsive reaction to "genital danger." This mode of reaction is present in all cases of compulsion neurosis. Sometimes its effect is seen in character traits or in the symptoms.

Whereas normally aggression in a man serves his genitality, the relationship is reversed in the compulsion neurotic, in whom sexual excitation serves the destructive drive. The phallus is no longer the mediator of genital love and pleasure; it has become (in extreme cases) a lethal weapon. For the aggressive male compulsive character, coitus primarily signifies stabbing or drilling through a woman. The results of this pathological attitude vary according to the rest of the individual character structure.

1. *Abstinence based on ascetic ideology.* Typical rationalizations are that sexual intercourse is dirty (anal) and animalistic (sadistic). Phallic sadism emerges as hyper-

---

[3] This case history dates from 1923. At that time I did not know that the compulsion to eat is a means of suppressing vegetative sensations in the abdomen. Today I would handle the case differently.

morality, and anality as hyperestheticism. This ideology of course collapses as soon as sexual anxiety reemerges. The sexual act had simply been resisted on the principle of "sour grapes."

2. *Erective impotence.* This does not occur frequently in compulsion neurotics, although in this context it has a significance different than in hysteria. In the latter, erective impotence is caused merely by fear of excitation, whereas in the former there is an "erection taboo," the purpose of which is to avoid an unconsciously fantasized murder with a lethal weapon, the "phallus." This may be seen in individual symptoms as well as in dreams and fantasies, in which patients tend to select firearms and stabbing weapons as genital symbols; their sexual daydreams always involve the idea of raping a woman struggling to resist. Sadistic impulses are either toward women directly (the mother) or have merely been carried over from sadistic impulses against men (the father). When compulsion neurosis is coupled with a noticeable turning away from women toward men, then the phallic-sadistic impulse also signifies homosexual aggression.

The developmental phases of these two forms of compulsion-neurotic impotence are as follows: incest desires and hate of the father (hysterical), resulting in fear of castration by the father; flight to the anal-sadistic stage, where the castration danger is resisted through (anal) sadistic aggression toward the father, which always essentially signifies (phallic) castration of the father; fear of being punished (castrated) for this offense; renewed sadistic resistance to the danger; strong repression and reaction-formation against the phallic aggression through introjection of the prohibiting, punishing father; transformation of fear of the father into guilt feelings (the ego's fear of the super-ego). In compulsion neurosis one usually unmasks genital anxiety only after anal and phallic sadism have been exposed and the rationalizations for disdaining sex have been removed. In hysteria, genital anxiety lies close to the surface.

3. *Extreme reduction of orgastic potency despite good erective and ejaculative potency.* Next to asceticism, this is the most frequent form of compulsion-neurotic impotence. In cases of this kind the potency disturbance is easily overlooked because of the patient's adequate erective capacity. It was just such cases that were cited as objections against my claim that there are no neuroses without disturbances of the genital function. However, one need only inquire carefully about sexual sensations during intercourse or analyze the general attitude toward the sexual act to be convinced of the presence of severe disturbances that give rise to sexual stasis.

For many conscientious compulsion neurotics, sexual intercourse is merely a marital duty during which they must strain to master their feelings of impotence. One such patient had sexual relations according to a schedule, and, whenever coitus was due, had to repeat to himself all day, "Today I must engage in intercourse, I must not forget." Another patient, previously mentioned, had intercourse frequently, just "for practice." After completing several listless thrusts, he would desist, having convinced himself that he was still potent. He had "practiced" intercourse in this fashion for two decades and, in addition to his pseudopotency and compulsion neurosis, had also manifested typical symptoms of acute neurasthenia.

All such cases have in common a lack of sexual desire usually coupled with a more or less pronounced impairment of penis sensitivity. So-called cold erections are extremely common in compulsion neurotics and are characterized by a lack of the specific sensation of pleasurable tension. Because of the lack of pleasure sensations (i.e., of electrical charge produced through friction) that normally bring on the discharge of semen, persons suffering from this disorder either have great difficulty in ejaculating or do not ejaculate at all.

Orgastic impotence in erectively potent compulsion neurotics is easily recognized. Compulsive brooders dwell on their problems during intercourse; compulsive counters count their thrusts; compulsive ritualists anxiously attempt to keep to a certain order even during intercourse, or fear they have neglected some detail of their coital ceremonials. Pleasure sensations, which are weak to begin with, hardly increase in intensity during ejaculation, if, indeed, ejaculation occurs at all. (In some cases the disturbance of sensitivity is connected with premature ejaculation.) Intercourse is followed by leaden fatigue, guilt, boredom, or disgust.

Typically, compulsive characters recognize their illness only when their compulsive systems, despite all efforts to extend them, can no longer control the sexual stasis. This, in turn, causes stasis anxiety or neurasthenic states of fatigue, headaches, work disturbances, insomnia, and the like.

Not infrequently, compulsion-neurotic abstinence begins after a fiasco in the form of erective or ejaculative impotence. In such cases the purpose of abstinence is unmistakable, namely, self-deception regarding feelings of impotence. In contrast to hysterics and chronic neurasthenics, compulsion neurotics usually pay little or no attention to their impotence or, in spite of clear evidence, do not even admit it to themselves. However, the repressed feeling of impotence soon emerges as a feeling of general inferiority. In common with compulsion neurotics, some phallic-narcissistic characters also manifest

this nonrecognition of, and compensation for, impotence.

Whereas the male compulsion-neurotic character remains masculinely active (in contrast to the male
hysteric), and the female hysterical character maintains a
feminine attitude, the female compulsive character is
predominantly masculine-aggressive. The explanation of
this is provided by analysis of the compulsion-neurotic
form of frigidity, which is all the more total the more pronounced the compulsive character is. The desire to possess
a penis not only expresses itself in sexual peculiarities and
in fantasies, as in hysterical characters, but it also influences the character in the sense of ego masculinization:
not only does the female compulsive character want to be
a man; she easily succeeds in behaving like a man and
fulfilling masculine ideals. In this case, the correlate to rejection of men is a strong emphasis on homosexual striving
in the role of a man as opposed to the tendency in female
hysterics, caused by disappointments in men, to develop
an infantile, passive submission to women.

Female hysterics affirm and even exaggerate the femininity of their character, since their anxiety relates only to
genital excitation. Compulsion-neurotic women reject
femininity altogether and are thus constrained to compensate with exaggerated masculinity. Since they have
become men characterologically, the acceptance of men as
love objects would remind them of their anatomically imposed fate. For this reason they not only reject men but
continually assert their own masculinity. They use sadism,
which is nourished by their lack of satisfaction, as a means
to assist them in this endeavor. Their intent (which usually remains unconscious) is to rob the man of his penis,
partly in order to possess it themselves, and partly to
eliminate the organ that would be capable of evoking

their repressed but not-yet-deadened female yearnings. (We recall here the case of chronic depression previously described.) Thus, one may also observe that in many female compulsion neurotics, symptomatic illness is caused by a relaxation of the repression of genital sexuality—an acute infatuation, the loss, through death or marriage, of an unconsciously loved, although consciously rejected, man, and the like. The sadistic defense against genital danger is expressed through the symptoms.

Whereas sadism in male compulsion neurotics most frequently retains its phallic nature, sadism in female compulsion neurotics is strongly anal in nature, the majority of cases being characterized by fantasies of trampling, "squashing to a pulp," crushing underfoot, striking on the buttocks, etc.

It is obvious that this character system in compulsive women represents merely a reactive superstructure built up over their basic femininity; this is proven by the character transformation that one sees in such cases when they undergo character analysis. The feminine attitude reveals itself just as automatically as it does in hysteria, although with greater difficulty. However, instead of resisting these impulses with anxiety, as the hysteric does, the compulsive patient does so with hate, until somewhere, unmistakably, a feminine attitude finally breaks through. Usually this new phase is initated by hysteriform anxiety, which simply means that the compulsion neurosis is beginning to be transformed into hysteria. Dynamically expressed, the anxiety has been freed from the symptoms that had previously bound it. Further indications of this change are spontaneously occurring genital sensations that frighten the patient. They indicate that genital anxiety, which heretofore had been quite inconspicuous, is now also emerging. The intent to destroy the dangerous object that arouses genital impulses has been replaced by resistance toward the impulses themselves. The object is allowed to remain; it has been accepted. The therapeutic goal has been accomplished when the genital anxiety released from the compulsive symptoms has been eliminated.

Genital Asthenia in Chronic Hypochondriacal Neurasthenia

In a brief paper on chronic hypochondriacal neurasthenia,[4] I attempted, within the framework of the psychoanalytic theory of neurosis, to distinguish between compulsion neurosis and a group of illnesses that, though they manifest the same pregenital fixation, are fundamentally different in character, symptomatology, and form of potency disturbance. In that article I dealt primarily with the morphological and psychogenetic differences between this group and compulsion neurosis and hysteria. Now I should like to discuss in detail the specific nature of the potency disturbance, which I termed "genital asthenia." It is never encountered in hysteria or compulsion neurosis but is a characteristic symptom of chronic hypochondriacal neurasthenia.

A twenty-nine-year-old student sought treatment for impotence. A period of frequent nocturnal emissions had followed several years of masturbation begun when he was twenty-two. Although masturbation initially had taken place only once or twice a week, this rate was soon moderated, whereupon the patient began to experience spermatorrhea and urinary seepage. He had first dared sexual encounters when he was twenty-five, but as soon as

---

[4] In *Internationale Zeitschrift für Psychoanalyse*, XII, 1926.

he even touched a woman, ejaculation always occurred—
as a mere flow, with the penis remaining completely flaccid. No genuine attempt at coition was ever undertaken,
nor had the patient ever had an erection. Two years
before treatment, he had had one experience in which a
very aggressive girl persuaded him to go to bed with her.
On this occasion, he resisted removing his underpants, remained utterly unaroused, and finally, turned his back to
the girl and fell asleep facing the wall. Since then he had
never again allowed matters to go so far, contenting himself with meager ejaculation in his clothes.

Other symptoms, which had arisen during a compar-
atively untroubled puberty, were occasional headaches,
nausea, and a sensation of oppression in the chest. The patient was always in a bad mood. He was capable of work
but very susceptible to physical fatigue and was frequently
unable to read or to compute figures for any length of
time. For several years he had also been suffering in his
back and limbs from rheumatic aches that were not influenced by the weather or alleviated by any treatment.
They were irregular, diffuse hypochondriacal sensations.
Furthermore, as far as he could remember, he had always
suffered from severe constipation. Only certain laxatives
or sitting on a pot filled with hot water would bring relief.
A physical examination was negative, with the exception
of varicosities of the left leg.

All members of the immediate family (i.e., parents and
three older siblings) also suffered from constipation. With
the exception of his father, a compulsive, ambivalent character, the entire family was well adjusted. The patient
himself was a timid and depressed, although extremely af-
fable, person whose bearing betrayed a passive-feminine
character.

As early as the second session he reported a dream, the

manifest content of which profoundly frightened him. He dreamed he had kissed the genitalia of his sister, who was five years older than he. It was not so much the act itself that shocked him as the fact that it involved his sister. All he could say was that he had been particularly fond of this sister since childhood and that his love was returned. Several years before, she had married in a foreign country and taken residence there, resigned in a quiet union. The patient visited her frequently. Their relationship was intimate to the extent that she shared her marital secrets with him, including complaints about her frigidity. During puberty they had sworn to live together at some later date and never to leave each other. She had always been his motherly advisor and encouraged his younger-brother attitude.

In a subsequent session, he reported the recent recall of a phobia from the period between the ages of four and seven. The description of the object of his fear was extremely fragmentary. Whenever he entered the dimly lit foyer in his house, he had a vision: a "ghost" (as he had called it at the time) came "climbing down from somewhere up above," or seemed to be "emerging from someone," or appeared "as if a shirt had been pulled over the head." For the moment no further information could be obtained.

Immediately after relating the dream involving his sister, the patient informed me with great reticence that between the ages of four and six he had engaged in sexual play with a girl cousin five years older than he. With the exception of several significant details, this had never been repressed, and the memory had always burdened him. He felt these games had been the most wicked acts of his life and traced his illness exclusively to them. The games had mainly consisted of playing doctor and patient, including inspecting and touching each other's anus and genitalia. He remembered very clearly that he had touched her genitalia but did not know whether she had manipulated his. Kisses were prescribed as treatment for various parts of the body. Much later he recalled, with obvious disgust, that there had also been mutual kissing of the anal fold. Usually the active part was taken by his cousin, who behaved exactly like a boy in other respects as well. In the patient's opinion, the disturbing aspect of the games lay in the fact that they had determined his later masturbation fantasies, which never contained the idea of coitus. His favorite fantasies involved being tied, touching the female parts with his tongue, and sucking on a breast. Later he dreamed and fantasized that his penis was being sucked and that he was licking feces out of the anus. Before the latter fantasy became conscious, he suffered through a long period of intense morning nausea. He also recalled the peculiar enjoyment he derived, as a child, from sitting at his mother's feet and then crawling between her legs and trying to come as close to her genitalia as possible with his head. At a much later date a memory surfaced that gave considerable support to my speculation that his mother was the actual object of his anal-oral desires. He saw himself in the bedroom, very small, watching his mother wash her breasts and genitalia.

The question of how he had manipulated his own genitalia remained unanswered. The idea of passive fellatio occurred in his fantasies, but he could not recall anything pertaining to it, in contrast to his clear recollection of other events. We shall postpone the question of his genital manipulation until we have clarified the motives and object of his childhood fear.

The first elements of the ghost to be seen clearly were that (1) it was climbing down from somewhere; (2) it was as if it were emerging from someone; (3) it was as if it had been pulled over the head like a shirt. Very soon after reporting this long-forgotten vision, the patient realized what had occasioned his sudden recall of it. His little cousin had pulled the "soul"* out of a soccer ball, and the memory had appeared like a flash. This trivial experience had an ecphorizing effect for two reasons, one of which was immediately obvious. The ghost was reddish, naked, and bald. The drawing the patient made at my request represented a young man whom he immediately recognized as his brother, who was approximately ten years older than he. Further associations led to the memory that his brother had once frightened him severely. However, he was unable to cite the occasion, so this recollection was of no help in clarifying the three elements above. It was only when the patient remembered that the lining of the soccer ball was made of red rubber that he spontaneously understood the first element ("it is climbing down from somewhere"). This involved a douche and enema bag with a red rubber tube. It also occurred to him that occasionally it had seemed as if the ghost emerged from a muff lying on a cabinet in the foyer. But a newly surfaced memory that the douche usually lay on a high shelf in the bathroom contradicted this. Taking into consideration the fact that he had observed his mother washing herself, the idea of the muff in connection with the third element ("it is pulled over the head like a shirt") could signify only one thing: he must have observed his mother engaged in vaginal douching (the muff as a vagina symbol), for which purpose she probably removed her slip.

But what role did the brother play, and why did the douche bag appear as such a terrifying ghost?

The material below, which the patient recalled

* Colloquial German for the inner rubber lining. [Trans.]

gradually over the course of many months, assisted in finding answers to these questions.

The following is a dream from the beginning of this period: "I am kneeling in a church with several others, praying, with my head bowed down to the ground. When I leave, there is an immense ghostlike form standing in front of the door; I am frightened to death." His first association was that he had prayed like a Mohammedan, bowing deeply to the floor (church?). The spontaneous recollection then emerged that as a child he had always said *Kristier* instead of *Klistier*.* He had suffered from constipation at a very early age and had always been given enemas by his mother.[5] The prayer position in his dream was similar to the position assumed for an enema. There were numerous other proofs of the intensity of his anal excitement. He recalled that when he was about three years old, the family doctor had once asked jokingly, "Are you always sitting on the throne?" A prolonged period in his early childhood was spent playing with blocks, which he usually did while sitting on the potty. And whereas other children run around when playing railroad, our patient slid around the room on his potty. Later he was able to overcome his inability to evacuate only by sitting on a pot full of hot water. His mother gave him enemas and suppositories until he was eight, but later on he tolerated enemas only when the constipation was particularly persistent. Nevertheless, he frequently discussed matters of defecation with his mother, who showed a great interest in the subject.

As do many other constipated individuals, he used numerous rationalizations to postpone defecation. If, on

---

* Enema. [Trans.]

[5] In dreams the church is a mother symbol, and in this case also stands for the patient's *Kristier* (Christ).

occasion, he felt spontaneous intestinal urgency, he would always have more important things to do, just as he did as a child on the potty. An aversion to the toilet was also active here and was based on an early fear of the toilet bowl and the enema. As a boy, whenever he sat on the toilet, he always had to leave the door open and keep his back against the wall. Despite these precautions, he was extremely afraid that a "thing" (an object, ghost, or specter) might emerge from the bowl and do something to him.

The ghost was male and later bore the features of his brother. How then did the pleasurable anal relationship with his mother and the fear of his brother become intertwined? He had valued and admired his brother to the point of utter selflessness, particularly since adolescence. One can only compare his relationship with his brother to that of a teenager in love. He was overjoyed when his brother went for a walk with him and infinitely sad when he saw that his brother, so much older than he, preferred the company of others. Silently he accused the brother of not loving him enough. For him, the brother's advice and opinions were inviolable. The healthy, well-adjusted brother had severed his home ties at a very early age, because of the consistently uncongenial atmosphere. When the patient noticed that his brother was drifting away despite all his efforts, he withdrew, deeply insulted, and sought the company of men who were much like his brother. With conspicuous enjoyment and without hesitancy, he assumed the role of a follower looking up to his leader. However, during the course of treatment it became increasingly clear that this love and devotion was a reaction-formation. Only a few days after he started treatment, the patient had a thought that, initially, he paid no attention to: sitting in a café, lost in dreams, he had suddenly visualized an obituary announcement. In the ensuing days, at first vaguely and then with ever in-creasing clarity, he began to reproach his mother for preferring his brother to him. The brother had, indeed, been the mother's favorite, a fact that had been difficult for the patient to bear. "All mother talked about was H., H., and H. again" (i.e., the brother). He had to wear his brother's cast-off clothing and join in singing the praises of his intelligence, diligence, and good manners. The patient had not attempted to compete with his rival. Having often observed that his mother loved people who praised her favorite son and hated those who were against him, he had decided shortly before puberty (at about age eleven) to gain his mother's love by joining her in her admiration of the brother. However, the fact that he gradually slipped into immoderate adoration of his brother was the result of the repression of all negative impulses toward him, primarily the wish that he would die. Hence, his love for the brother was dictated by guilt feelings and was a reaction to his hate. The ghost could thus represent the brother in conjunction with the douche bag which, one might say, represented the mother's pleasure organ and the mother herself.

The second element of the ghost was that it seemed to be "emerging from someone." We recall that this memory had been triggered when the lining ("soul") of the soccer ball was pulled out. As a child the patient had imagined that death takes place when the soul, which he visualized as having the same form as the body, leaves the body. Therefore, the spirit or ghost haunting the patient was the soul of the deceased brother, that is, the brother whom he wished dead.

Following the exposure of the autoerotic pleasure the patient gained from his constipation and of the relation-ship to his mother, intestinal activity showed a marked improvement. However, the patient still suffered from severe cramps and colic accompanied by nausea and flatulence, and the final remission of constipation occurred only after further relationships were brought to light.

The analysis of a tendency to retain intestinal gas resulted in exposure of his pronounced pleasure in anal odors and of his reaction-formations to certain of his father's behavioral patterns. The patient had a very fine sense of smell. Several times in the course of treatment he hallucinated the odor of urine. His concern about flatulence was a reaction to his father, who never took pains to retain wind in the presence of his family. Since at a very early age the patient noticed his mother's condemnation of this behavior, he began, for love of her, to develop traits opposite to those of his father, just as, for the same reason, he later adored his brother. His father was stingy, indiscreet, opened every letter that came to the house, and was quarrelsome. The patient, on the contrary, paid no attention to money, and was especially discreet and agreeable. The father was without scruples in anal matters; the patient would not permit himself even to break wind. However, this denial in the name of love for his mother was not easily accomplished; it had required a considerable amount of suppression and produced tormenting organic symptoms. The mere exposure of these relationships caused the flatulence to disappear, and his general feeling of well-being improved.

Strangely, the colicky pain, which always occurred toward morning, persisted. Resolving this problem was far less successful, although the pain did disappear when pregnancy fantasies became conscious. The specific quality of the pain could not be explained,[6] but its connection

---

[6] (1937) This case history dates from 1924, a time when the connection between the infant's *fear* of defecation and the sympathetically induced states of intestinal contraction was as yet unknown to me. I have left this passage unaltered in order to show that at the time I was already aware of the manifest inadequacy

with the idea of having a feces-child in his abdomen was obvious, apart from its periodic nature. The patient's stool was formed of "tiny little pieces of stool," which he called "bobby." In this connection, he recalled the great childhood interest he had had in the goat droppings he saw when he went to the country in the summer. He compared them to olives, and the nausea that accompanied the reporting of these details during treatment was unequivocal evidence for the pronounced coprophagous tendencies underlying his dreams and experiences of anilingus. The following dream introduced this phase: "I am a child playing in a large room; gold coins are lying about; I defecate little pieces of stool which disappear and are replaced by tiny little children." The analysis of this dream did not reveal which unconscious idea was *more* significant, that of being stool himself, that is, the child in the large room (in the mother), or of actively bearing children himself. Very frequently the patient spoke of his defecation as a "difficult birth," although neither the exploration of his childhood nor the anamnesis offered evidence that he had ever observed a delivery. For this reason it was all the more peculiar that he recalled a period of intense brooding about the problem of procreation. Observation of animals and their young, when he was in the country, had played an important role. For some time around the age of four, he passed through a questioning period. He clearly remembered his disappointment with the answer he received to the question of what the word *Hebamme** meant. He was told it was a

---

of the psychological explanation of organ symptoms. It was this very inadequacy of the purely psychoanalytic interpretation that forced me to search for a relation between instinctual affects and vegetative functions. Today it is clear: chronic constipation is the result not of pregnancy fantasies but of defecation anxiety. The fantasies reflect the merging of experience with physiologically determined organ sensations that are already present.
*Literal German, "midwife." [Trans.]

female greengrocer, but he knew better. He knew that the stomach containing the child opened, and that the *Amme** gave her breast to the child who became attached to it through sucking and was thus lifted out of the stomach.†

At the time the patient's nocturnal colic was most severe and he was suffering from diurnal headaches and nausea, his dreams centered around the idea of being orally fertilized by the doctor. One such dream was as follows: "The plumber is repairing our pipes and I am with him; suddenly he starts a rinsing machine; the liquid sprays out like a fine vapor (*I become wet*) and tastes salty." His associations to the first part of the dream immediately indicated that the plumber represented the analyst repairing the pipes, that is, the patient's penis. The second part contained both the affective resistance against being cured of impotence and the fulfillment of a preferred wish, namely, that the analyst fertilize him (an association) orally with urine (salty taste). This also explained the olfactory hallucinations. The patient recalled having smelled urine on the genitalia of his cousin during their sexual games. It remained uncertain whether either of them had actually urinated. Thus, the olfactory hallucinations during the treatment sessions not only were recollections of the games but also represented wishes directed toward the analyst's urinary apparatus. The pipes in his dream also had a determinant from childhood: he had been very interested in the bathroom pipes (especially the toilet pipe) before fear of the enema and toilet bowl began. The meaning of this interest was first clarified through analysis of the following dream: "An eagle carries a woman off into the air, then drops her on me." The

---

*Literal German, "wet nurse" or "nurse." [Trans.]

†German *heben*, "to lift"; thus the patient's interpretation of *Hebamme*. [Trans.]

eagle is his father, the woman, his mother; the abduction into the sky represents parental coitus. When attempting coitus during the period of treatment, the patient had to struggle against a desire to lie under the woman and approach her genitalia with his mouth. The idea that the mother fell on him after coitus with the father fit exactly into his anal relationship to his mother with her enema bag. Several days before the dream mentioned above, he dreamed he was having intercourse lying beneath a prostitute who had a penis; that is, the mother was having intercourse with him using the father's penis. Behind the passive-anal relationship to his mother there existed the same relationship to the father. The elder brother thus represented not only the mother with the enema but also the father. All this was worked through on an entirely anal level. And now we also know toward whom the death wishes expressed in the phobia were directed. During the analysis of these relationships the patient blurted out, "I will be potent only when my father is dead."

The brother became in a decisive way the representative of the father for another reason as well. As we have seen, almost all the patient's sexual strivings derived from oral and urethral eroticism, were passive-anal in nature, and were dominant from earliest childhood. So we must now ask what became of the genital strivings. For a year and a half there was no mention of them in analysis. Only toward the end of treatment did a chain of associations lead to a castration threat experienced by the patient. The following dream enabled us to reconstruct an important scene: "I am playing the piano in a dark room. In an adjoining room Dr. S. [an Austrian statesman] is delivering a speech and is elevated in some way. He is angrily glaring at me through his glasses." Dr. S.'s profile reminded the patient of his brother, who also wore glasses, and the memory that his brother liked to walk on stilts in the country fit together with "elevated." In addition, a vague memory of a gloomy hallway and the fear experienced there emerged. The day before he had this dream, the brother had asked me how analysis was progressing, and the patient had wondered for a moment whether I might tell the brother something about the content of the analysis. Moreover, at the outset of treatment the patient had asked me not to tell his brother that he had masturbated. If we take the piano-playing in the dream (a typical masturbation symbol), together with the speech (scolding) and the angry glare, it is a reasonable hypothesis that the brother once caught our patient manipulating his genitalia in a dark hallway (foyer ghost?) and scolded him. This must have happened very early, at about age three, because the memory of the ghost began after he had turned four, and the scene must have preceded the phobia. Thus, the fear of the ghost bearing the brother's features was based, in the final analysis, on that original scene in which the brother had precipitated castration fears.

In this connection there emerged a faint memory that the cousin had pulled the patient's testicles during their games. The characteristic pain persisted in that region, as a reminder, so to speak. Furthermore, this corresponded to the patient's stereotyped complaints that it was not his penis but his testicles that were too small, and to his timidity about undressing completely in a woman's presence.

With the exception of this one memory, the analysis, although exposing early childhood sexual activities and fantasies in great detail, yielded not the slightest evidence that genitality had ever played a particular role. Urethral eroticism was less prominent than anal eroticism, but it did emerge clearly in ejaculatio praecox and in the olfactory hallucinations. We should add that, as a child, the patient enjoyed being in the bathroom and playing with water. But even this first evidence of genitality was worked through anally and orally. The interest in pipes served both anal and urethral tendencies.

It is now clear how the patient fantasized himself as the object of urethral relationships (being splashed with urine, i.e., being fertilized by the analyst; approaching the female genitalia with his mouth) and mixed them with fantasies of sucking. Prominent among the memories that surfaced during analysis was his seeing cows being milked. Equating the udder with the penis led to, first, his fantasies of sucking on the genitalia and on a woman's breast and, second, his equating his own penis with the breast (or udder) and the semen or urine with milk. When a female body was touched, semen flowed out. In keeping with his feminine character, the penis had been enlisted as a breast. Masturbation consisted not of manual stroking but of pressing the flaccid penis against an object. According to my experience, this is a typical indication that the penis represents the desired breast. It is as if the object were being shown what one desires oneself.

Genital excitation was blocked. As a result of the general sexual stasis, anal, oral, and urethral excitation pressed all the more insistently for discharge, flooding all psychic functions. The genitals themselves had entered the service of nongenital forms of excitation. Because of the blocking of genital excitation in early childhood, secondary, unnatural impulses had become rampant. The patient tried to control these by tidiness and pedantry. The genital asthenia he had incurred diminished his self-confidence and kept him in an attitude of childish femininity toward superior men.

The pregenital states of excitation strengthened the entire defense mechanism without any corresponding discharge and equalization. Nongenital impulses can only accumulate; they can never provide satisfaction. This constitutes their fundamental distinction from genital excitation.

Manifestations of puberty, which usually occur between the ages of twelve and fourteen, first appeared in the patient when he was twenty-two. At this time he began to practice masturbation involving pregenital fantasies and suffered severe guilt feelings and fears that later led to restraint. The spermatorrhea and urinary seepage were evidence of permanent overstimulation. The pregenital mechanisms involved nonorgastic disposal of the excitation.

When, because of rising sexual excitation, the patient had attempted intercourse, his pregenital structure immediately interfered: he pressed his genitalia against the woman, ejaculated a mild flow of semen, and then turned his back to her in the unconscious expectation of receiving an enema. Genital excitation was barred from the genital apparatus, which had grown accustomed to pregenital excitation.

Analysis did manage to relieve the obstipation. The headaches disappeared; the pressure in the patient's chest proved to be an anxiety symptom and, without its specific determination being traced, also disappeared in the course of analysis. Spermatorrhea, urinary seepage, and the pollutions upon contact with a woman also ceased. Following exposure of the castration scene, the patient twice succeeded in having intercourse. However, genital excitation remained weak; he had no desire for coitus.

In the first edition of this book, I concluded the report as follows:

This patient's constitution was beyond the limits of analysis. What had not developed in childhood could not be manufactured. Analysis can deal only with drive impulses that are already present; it can subsequently rearrange these, but it can never add anything to them. A more objective attitude toward his mother and a certain indifference toward his father and brother proved that analysis had been as successful as was possible. The patient also became less inhibited in general. Naturally this success was hardly able to compensate for the genital disability, although it did make it more bearable. That further analysis might have achieved more cannot be discounted, although this is very improbable in view of the patient's libido structure.

How easily one takes refuge in the explanation "unalterable constitution," when, in fact, it is only a matter of insufficient knowledge! Since that time I have succeeded in comprehending the genital-spastic attitudes that underlie genital asthenia. This has made it possible to cure several cases of severe genital asthenia. In the foregoing case history I also had to make changes wherever I had given a psychological explanation for disturbances of organic function. The displacement of nongenital forms of excitation onto the genitals causes particular kinds of sexual behavior. The patient's severe ejaculatio praecox was an expression of his genital asthenia. This potency disturbance is characteristic of severe forms of chronic neurasthenia.

Two Forms of Ejaculatio Praecox

The term "ejaculatio praecox" is used to designate that form of genital disturbance in which semen is discharged prematurely. Depending on the manner in which the premature discharge occurs, two basic forms of ejaculatio praecox may be distinguished, one caused by *genital asthenia* and the other by *genital anxiety.*

The following clinical differences have led to this distinction:

1. Ejaculatio praecox exists from the outset; or it occurs only after a period of relative potency.
2. Premature seminal discharge occurs *before* penetration of the penis; or it occurs only *after* penetration.
3. The premature seminal discharge occurs as a flow; or it occurs in bursts.
4. During seminal discharge the penis is always *flaccid*; or it is always *erect.*
5. The sensitivity of the penis is greatest internally, within the urethra; or it is greatest externally, on the glans.
6. The idea of penile penetration is replaced by pregenital fantasies (snuggling up to the woman, kissing her breasts, being bound, etc.); or sexual fantasies, conscious or unconscious, are dominated by the idea of the penis penetrating the vagina, whether or not this idea is pleasurable.

The above characteristics usually fall together, respectively, into two groups. In one, ejaculation before penetration is generally connected with a smooth streaming of semen, a more or less flaccid penis, and pregenital fantasies. In the other, in which there is erective potency, seminal discharge shortly after penetration is occasionally rhythmical and always connected with active coitus fantasies. Exceptions do exist, chiefly those instances of erective potency in which ejaculation occurs before penetration. Experience confirms that as a rule the first form is far

more severe and usually chronic, whereas the second occurs most frequently following a period of relatively good
potency and reacts very well to vegetotherapy.

The difference lies in an essential dissimilarity of sexual
structure. In the severe form, genital excitability has given
way entirely to *non*genital mechanisms; in the mild form
it has been retained physiologically and psychologically.
The presence of pure genital excitation is manifested by:

1. The ability to have an erection.
2. The glans being more excitable than the urethra
   or the root of the penis.
3. The presence of coitus fantasies.
4. The character of patients with the milder form is
   masculine, active, and aggressive, and they are
   sometimes overt homosexuals. The illness started
   after a period of relative potency.

The absence of genital excitability in ejaculatio praecox,
or a predominance of anal excitation, is shown by the following characteristics:

1. The patient was never potent.
2. Heterosexual coitus fantasies are absent altogether
   or they are overshadowed by pregenital fantasies.
   (One, of course, must not be led astray by the patient's expressing the wish for treatment in order
   to become able to have intercourse. The unconscious fantasies are what matter.)
3. The glans is either only very slightly excitable or
   not excitable at all (penile hypesthesia or anesthesia). Pleasure sensations are localized in the
   urethra and almost always extend into the peri-
   neal region.

4. Erection is negligible, does not occur at all, or is suddenly lost.
5. The character of the patient is passive-feminine and usually masochistic. In addition, he almost always manifests neurasthenic symptoms, such as chronic constipation, headaches, lack of energy, spermatorrhea, and hypochondriacal ailments.

The genesis of the two forms is different in that the more severe form is usually caused by *primary fixation at a pregenital stage;* whereas in the milder form, genital excitation exists but is bound by anxiety. In ejaculatio praecox at the genital stage, the normal *genital* attachment to the mother was adversely affected by castration anxiety. However, a strong phallic position upheld the father identification and prevented masculinity from being relinquished. In some cases there is also castration anxiety in relation to the mother, manifested as fear of some dangerous "thing" (i.e., the father's penis) in the vagina, or the inhibiting idea that the vagina is armed with teeth that might bite off the penis. The joy of urinating served genital and exhibitionistic tendencies and is often also the reason for the pleasure taken in the seminal flow. Hence, in such cases, ejaculatio praecox is an expression of the fear (sometimes conscious) of "entering the lion's den" (as one patient expressed it) and is also a protection against having to stay there very long. In this sense the premature discharge of semen may be likened to diarrhea or involuntary loss of urine in certain children when they experience anxiety or fear. Occasionally, behind the father identification, which gives the masculine-aggressive stamp to the character, there is a mother identification, at a genital level, which does not stifle the father identification. The vegetative excitation directed toward the genitals does indeed occur, but the anxiety that immediately sets in provokes a short-circuit-like discharge through premature contractions of the genital musculature. However, the excitation remains essentially directed toward the genital region.

Matters are quite different when ejaculation before penetration occurs with a flaccid penis. In my experience such cases usually involve a developmental inhibition and a primary fixation of sexual development at the anal-urethral stage. I know of only one case where complete regression from the genital to the anal stage could be proven. Fixation at the pregenital level entails an absence of genital desire; instead, there is a urethral relationship to women (mother) and a passive-anal relationship to men (father). Anal and urethral satisfactions are usually manifest, without the patient necessarily being aware of them. Whereas in genital-stage ejaculatio praecox, genital anxiety is predominant, the anal form is dominated by autoerotic satisfaction or by the desire to soil the woman with urine or feces. Micturition and defecation are invested with intense interest. One patient, for instance, spent hours on the toilet, allowing his excrement to move out slowly, piece by piece. He frequently avoided having a bowel movement for as many as eight days in order to be able to remove the hardened feces with his finger. Two other patients, in whom it had been possible to uncover some slight genital excitation and a desire for coitus, when approaching a woman, tense with anticipation of what was to come, would instead go to the toilet. After defecation, all "desire for coitus" had disappeared. In cases of this kind, the vegetative excitation is deflected to the rear. An overload of genital excitation gives rise to intense anxiety that forbids the excitation access to the front. Many patients in this category keep the small of the back perpetually arched and the pelvis retracted, thereby restricting the excitation. Almost all cases of precoital intestinal excitation are caused by excitation that has been deflected to the anal region.

While in the genital form of ejaculatio praecox, the major therapeutic work is completed once genital anxiety has been eliminated, in genital asthenia, success can be achieved only if the patient has been able to overcome the anxiety that prevents the forward movement of excitation. Excitation to the rear usually disappears of its own accord when this has happened.

In the fantasies of the genital asthenic the penis has become a breast and the semen has become milk. The penis is offered to the woman as the breast was once offered to the child. In fantasies and during foreplay the typical desire is to press oneself against the woman or to snuggle up to her. In the most serious cases this triggers the flow of semen. The patient plays a double game. Having renounced, or never having assumed, a masculine role, he surrenders to the woman (mother) as a child, and desires her breast. The fantasy of sucking on the breast is typical in such cases. (In one case I treated, the semen was discharged while the patient was sucking on his girl friend's breast.) At the same time he plays the role of the mother offering her breast to a child; it is as though he were showing the woman what he desires from her. Thus, sucking on the breast and the discharge of semen supplement each other and form an expression of the desire to be suckled. One patient believed that his semen was in his penis and that he could simply press it out. Semen and urinary seepage, which are so frequently combined with the severe form of ejaculatio praecox, are associated with the idea that the patient's own penis is the desired breast from which milk is flowing. One such patient, as a boy, delighted in offering his penis to his playmates to be sucked. Another patient sucked his own penis. He was playing mother and child simultaneously.

In genital asthenia, genitalia, urethra, and perineum are in a state of perpetual excitation. It makes little sense to say that the genital organs themselves are impaired. Was this impairment present from the beginning? In the opinion of urologists, overexcitation of the genital apparatus and ejaculatio praecox are the result of constant hyperemia of the genitals and hypertrophy of the prostate. But it is the other way round: chronic hyperemia is the result of the particular way these patients achieve sexual satisfaction. Under normal circumstances, acute hyperemia occurs in the genitals during foreplay and then disappears immediately following orgasm. But because those who suffer from genital asthenia are orgastically impotent, there is a perpetual urge to sexual excitation and, consequently, constant hyperemia. The hyperemia, the origin of which was psychogenic, causes, when it has become chronic, a lasting somatic change in the genitals.

Whereas genital satisfaction remains the actual goal in genital-stage ejaculatio praecox, foreplay constitutes the main objective in the pregenital form, inasmuch as those suffering from this form have renounced coitus. Since the penis has ceased to be the expression and instrument of masculinity, it serves an unconsciously desired femininity as an imagined breast. In this sense one might speak of an oral erotization of the penis (as the counterpart to hysterical genitalization of the oral zone). Genital asthenia is thus the result of a flooding of the genitals with pregenital excitation. It must be differentiated from the other forms of impotence in which genital impulses are centered in the genitals but are inhibited. The unconscious basic formula of impotence due to genital asthenia is "I do not wish to have sexual intercourse but prefer to use my genitals in such and such a way." In cases of simple impotence it would read "I wish to have sexual intercourse but will not do so because I am afraid."

The result of pregenital activation of the genitals is that the excitation, which can be discharged only through orgasm, takes hold of the rest of the body. Continual sexual stimulation augments this effect and results in hypochondriacal ailments. It should therefore be understood that the latter are not "figments of the imagination" but are, rather, well-substantiated *physical* disturbances. The neurasthenic's physical states of excitation and fatigue and his inability to work, as well as his perpetual urgency and sense of being under pressure, are all the results of genital asthenia.

Because of their genital asthenia and orgastic impotence, neurasthenics develop a specific character structure. The study of sexual stasis is of great theoretical importance for the study of character development. In patients suffering from sexual stasis we can observe that there is no psychic impulse without physical resonance, and that no physical process occurs without a consequent psychic reaction. Stasis neuroses show us the way to a biological basis common to both physical and psychic reactions.

CHAPTER SIX

On the Psychoanalytic Theory of Genitality

Pre-psychoanalytic psychology was unable to formulate the problem of the development of genital tendencies because it was working from the premise that the sexual instinct "awakens" during puberty as a result of somatic developmental processes, that is, that it emerges all at once, not merely as an internal impulse but also as a will directed toward a heterosexual object in the outside world. Freud was the first to differentiate between drive aim and drive object and, in addition, to confirm the existence of pregenital sexual phases through which libido passes during the first years of life, before the pregenital tendencies are consolidated and become subject to genital primacy. The question then arose whether pregenital forms of sexuality are simply replaced by genital forms or actually contribute, somehow, to the creation of genital primacy. This question involved not only the development of physiological sensitivity in the genital erogenous zone but also the problems of how the child's mental attitudes and experiences participate in this process and which motives form the basis for heterosexual object selection. Thus, a distinction must be made between a number of specific issues: the emergence of genital excitation (drive goal); the development of psychogenital object love (drive object); and the genetic relationship between the two (interrelationship between drive and experience).

Freud's original view was that genital primacy does not exist prior to puberty and that the pregenital partial drives are brought under the primacy of the genitals only during puberty.[1] Later he revised this theory,[2] stating that genital primacy was established in childhood during the so-called phallic phase of libido development. This occurs in both sexes in the same manner: in men, penis pride arises as the most powerful support of male self-confidence; in women, penis envy is the basis of female inferiority feelings and of the compensations for them.[3] Here, "masculinity exists but not femininity; the opposites are male genitalia or castrated genitalia.[4] Only when this development is completed, during puberty, does sexual polarity coincide with the concepts of 'male' and 'female.' "[5] Boys retain the tendencies of this phase, whereas girls, after recognizing the inferiority of the clitoris, must mobilize other erogenous qualities in order to establish vaginal primacy and transfer clitoral eroticism to the vagina, a process which is finally completed only under favorable circumstances of development and only after puberty. According to the concurring views of numerous authors, the

---

[1] *Three Contributions to the Theory of Sex.*

[2] *The Infantile Genital Organization of the Libido.*

[3] *Cf.* H. Deutsch, "Psychoanalyse der weiblichen Sexualfunktionen," *Neue Arbeiten zur Ärztlichen Psychoanalyse,* Nr. V, 1925.

[4] One female patient whose case history I published [in *Early Writings, Volume One*] recalled during analysis that at age three she had theorized that there were two sorts of boys: good boys and bad boys. As punishment for having touched their penises, the latter group, i.e., girls, had had their genitalia cut off.

[5] Freud, *Infantile Genital Organization of the Libido.*

vagina plays no role as an erogenous zone during childhood; and in the analysis of women, one finds no indications of vaginal masturbation, except in cases of very early
seduction to coituslike manipulation which causes the
vagina to be discovered as a pleasure organ.

In his most recent investigation,[6] Freud's point of departure was the question of why girls carry an attachment to
the mother into the genital phase, just as boys do, and
then turn to their fathers. In boys the question is less complicated, since they do not need to change their original
object but merely pass from a relatively passive attitude in
the pregenital phase to an active one in the phallic phase.
Girls, however, not only become as active as boys but also
change their object. As causes for a loosening of attachment to the mother and the shift toward the father, Freud
cites the following:

1. Dissolution of attachment to the mother is frequently initiated by jealousy of another sibling
   whom the mother prefers.
2. The mother is held responsible for the lack of a
   penis; she "sent the child out into the world with
   inadequate equipment."[7]
3. Since, according to Freud, women in general are
   more adversely affected by masturbation than
   men, one may assume that this pleasurable activity is probably spoiled by the narcissistic slight of
   not having a penis and by "the admonition that
   girls are no match for boys in this and it is better

[6] "Some Psychological Consequences of the Anatomical Distinction Between
the Sexes," 1925.

[7] One of my female patients dreamed that she was in a room in which the
ceiling slowly began to descend. She knew that she now had to leave the room.
Once outside, she thought she had forgotten some longish object. She wanted to
rush back to fetch it but was already too late. The dream signified that she had
forgotten her penis in the womb at birth and wished to retrieve it.

therefore to avoid competition with them." Girls give up the desire for a penis and replace it with the desire for a child, selecting "the father as a love object with this intent." Hence, in girls, the castration complex introduces the Oedipus complex, whereas in boys the castration complex destroys the Oedipus complex.[8]

Freud does not indicate whether these motives for the female selection of a heterosexual object, which he found in several individual cases, have general validity. Although the previously cited experiences of little girls are typical and may therefore be counted among the normal preconditions for female sexual development, they do not appear to us to provide sufficient explanation of the later female attitude toward men.

Within the framework of psychological analysis, which should exceed individual limits only when forced to, we must differentiate carefully between "drive development" and the "development of relations to the external world." Although the latter are indeed based on instinctual attitudes, they nevertheless represent a higher level of drive development and, in addition, are primarily dependent upon the experiences themselves. "The origin of genitality" may imply either (a) the development of genital impulses or (b) the emergence of genital object love and object selection.

Methodologically speaking, there can be no objection to examining the origin of object love psychologically. Phallic eroticism, however, derives from physical stimulation, and therefore may be interpreted psychologically only in its psychic manifestations. Likewise, the sexual act itself is not subject to any one interpretation. It may, of

---

[8] *Cf.* Freud, *The Passing of the Oedipus Complex*, 1924.

course, be taken over by one tendency or another; for instance, it may be turned into an act of revenge or a proof of power, and can then be interpreted as a symptom. Nevertheless, it is a physiological act of pleasure, which, though it has attendant psychic symptoms and consequences, has no psychic *meaning* in itself.

Certainly it is impossible to accept Helene Deutsch's interpretation of the woman's sexual pleasure during intercourse as the high point of masochistic experience. And when, furthermore, the same author maintains that the ultimate female sexual pleasure is experienced in the act of giving birth, we are confronted with either a disturbing terminological inaccuracy or a supposition that is not substantiated by clinical facts. (Vaginal-masochistic patients are, without exception, extremely timid sexually and anesthetic in regard to intercourse.) We definitely feel that the high point of sexual pleasure is achieved in the sexual act (in women, through a vaginal orgasm).

In addition to methodological inaccuracies, such interpretations of the facts of genitality as Deutsch's are based on two errors. First, relationships encountered in severely ill persons are too readily employed to explain normal functioning, without due consideration being given to the extent, intensity, and form of instinctual life. Second, what is merely analogous is taken to be identical. The word "is," for example, and the word "signifies" are frequently used inaccurately in psychoanalysis. Even if they are not crucial in one context and may simply be termed inaccurate usage, in another context they may become a source of false claims and inextricable confusion. Normal coitus, for instance, supposedly "is," or "signifies," a regression to the womb. Obviously, the former cannot be literally true; and to say that coitus merely signifies this regression implies that although the individual consciously desires coitus, he unconsciously imagines a return to the womb. Here there has obviously been a carry-over from the area of the pathological to that of the normal. If an impotent patient dreams of coitus, he may be expressing a desire to return to the womb. But surely coitus itself is indicated when, for example, he dreams of crawling into a cave or fleeing into the womb, away from the castration he suspects awaits him in the sexual act. Overlooked here is the important fact that such an individual is impotent because for him coitus is not merely (or not at all) the satisfaction of autochthonous genitality in forepleasure and end pleasure but only, or predominantly, the satisfaction of his yearning for the womb, his oral libido, sadism, and so on. It has been firmly established that genital desires are regressively replaced by pregenital desires and a yearning for the womb when castration fear causes rejection of genital satisfaction.

In his *Versuch einer Genitaltheorie* Ferenczi has replaced the individual-psychological interpretation of coitus with a "bioanalytic" explanation. Methodologically there may be no objection to this. We have succeeded in clinically confirming part of his speculatively derived theory, namely, that ejaculation corresponds to the autotomy of an organ causing pain or tension. The heuristic value of many a "speculation" has been proved in this way. However, for the healthy individual, ejaculation does not signify castration. It is only for some neurotics that the orgasm signifies a danger (castration) and is thus disturbed. The normal sensation of "losing oneself" in the orgasm can occur only when one is free of castration anxiety.

Another group of Ferenczi's suppositions, those concerning the make-up of genitality, must be discussed in greater detail. Ferenczi attempted to explain the process of friction and ejaculation as the result of an amphimixis of anal and urethral drive impulses. Supposedly, ejaculation is a urethral process, and the prolongation of the friction period through retention of semen is an anal one. Normally, there is a sustained struggle between the desire to retain and the desire to discharge, with urethral eroticism finally emerging victorious. In ejaculatio praecox, however, urethral impulses are dominant from the beginning, and in impotentia ejaculandi anal impulses are dominant. Ferenczi contends that an equalization of these two tendencies is necessary for normal ejaculative potency to develop. In opposition to this, we must mention that ejaculation is entirely the result of a spinal reflex, which is set in motion through the sensory stimulus of friction. Friction itself can be as little explained psychologically as can an itch, unless one wishes to interpret physiological phenomena psychologically. However, Ferenczi viewed his interpretation merely as a point of departure for his promising "bioanalytic" hypothesis. In general, experience shows that nongenital functions can only disturb the genital function. Therefore, if Ferenczi's assumption is correct, there must be, in addition to the shift of anal and urethral qualities to the genitals, a factor that enables the normal genital function to develop. Do we not have to assume that in men it is phallic libido itself, with its own erogenous source, which is responsible for this transformation?

If the normal genital function of orgastically potent men is examined analytically, what is found, to varying degrees, and in addition to clear manifestations of phallic object love, are numerous other tendencies with which we are well acquainted from the analysis of impotent patients, those such as pregenital, sadistic wishes, and a yearning for the womb. Is it therefore possible, from the mere presence of such impulses, to draw conclusions concerning the genesis of the process or the "meaning" of a function? Certainly not, because some tendencies could have been added secondarily, following the formation of an already specifically determined function. When, for example, in healthy individuals the sadistic or oral tendency intensifies, the genital function suffers as a result. On the other hand, no changes are seen when genital pleasure or the orgastic experience is analyzed, so long as archaic incest wishes are not activated. Normally, genital eroticism is not in any way subjected to super-ego restrictions. From the standpoint of the super-ego, genitality may be tolerated, or even affirmed, but never rejected. It is readily demonstrated that even the fine differences between mere toleration and affirmation of genital satisfaction by the super-ego are expressed in the intensity of end pleasure and in the total attitude toward the sexual object as well as toward questions of sexuality. The pregenital eroticism, which is only secondarily included in normal genitality, and to an extent that varies from person to person, derives its satisfaction in forepleasure and end pleasure. Herein lies the subtlety of normal genitality. When repression or even simple resistance excludes pregenital demands from participation in genital satisfaction, genital satisfaction suffers to varying degrees, depending upon the intensity of the impulse involved and the resistance exerted against it. But what is the motive for this rejection?

It is unlikely that pregenital and other demands not belonging to genitality are allowed to participate in general sexual satisfaction unaltered, that is, uninfluenced by the genital tendency. This immediately becomes clear if one considers that if their actual goals were not altered in the normal sexual act, they would have a disturbing effect on the ego. The kiss, which begins the sexual act, certainly satisfies oral libido, the original drive goal of which was sucking. But when it is included in the sexual act it is raised to the genital level of satisfaction. The change from sucking to kissing may be attributed unreservedly to the influence of genitality on oral eroticism. This is best noted in tongue kissing. A contrary influence must certainly be assumed when the mouth makes contact with the partner's genitalia during foreplay. There exist all manner of transitional stages between this form of oral-genital contact and cunnilingus or fellatio as perversions with exclusive pregenital intentions. It should also be noted that the more insistent the pregenital demands the greater the impotence.

Anal eroticism loses its exclusive pregenital character when it is raised to the genital level in the form of coitus *a tergo* or olfactory eroticism. Urethral eroticism, in Ferenczi's sense, appears to be completely satisfied through ejaculation, due to its developmental relation to genitality. The pathological extreme is ejaculatio ante portas while the penis is flaccid. Here, urethral eroticism has taken exclusive possession of the genitals.

Thus, the "subordination of pregenital demands under genital primacy" during the phallic phase of libido development also causes a qualitative alteration of the partial drives. This must be attributed to the phallic character of libido and to the influence of early super-ego formation. One or another pregenital impulse may be excluded from genitalization due to partial fixation and isolated repression. Or, in the course of pubertal development of sexual activities, or even later, it may be suppressed once again and not allowed to participate in genital satisfaction. Such isolation, or partial repression, presents two dangers. First, a greater or lesser amount of libido is excluded from satisfaction and remains dammed up. The necessary countercathexis then detracts from the harmony of the sexual experience. Second, the repressed impulses constitute a refuge for tabooed desires; they are seeds from which neurosis may develop under suitable conditions. For example, a strict taboo against all coital positions except the "normal" one may be seen in compulsion neurotic characters with erective potency.

We have cited examples that illustrate how drastically the female orgasm may be disturbed by nongenitalized anal eroticism. The repressed drive demand would not, of itself, be able to produce a neurosis if it were not compounded by a general weakening of genital satisfaction and a resultant damming-up of libido. In this respect the taboos concerning manipulations that were once connected with the individual's masturbational activities are especially dangerous. A typical example is the taboo against mutual touching of the genitalia. This not only detracts from satisfaction but in women frequently produces vaginal anesthesia and in men causes extensive indifference toward the sexual act, if not a weakening of erective potency.

Having concluded this attempt to clarify the development of drive aims and their interrelationships, we shall return to the question of object selection.

Heterosexual object selection in boys does not in any way contradict drive goals during the various stages of libido development. The goals of oral as well as anal, urethral, and phallic libido are suited to the object that is closest to a boy from birth onward, namely, the mother, in the sense of an individually and biologically appropriate sexual attitude in later life. Through our previous summary of the conditions of libido development already known, and through clarification of the question of the "origin of genitality," we have established that the change in the erogenous relationship to this object poses no problem. Let us now turn to the question of object selection in girls.

In psychoanalytic literature two partly contradictory views may be found. One, advocated by Freud and H. Deutsch, contends that femininity in puberty, and its precursor, the loving attitude assumed by little girls toward their fathers, are formed through reaction. In other words, girls first develop in the direction of aggressiveness and masculinity and only secondarily change over to femininity. The other view, first emphasized by Karen Horney,[9] on the basis of her analyses, is that the denial of infantile wishes is highly significant for the development of the female castration complex, penis envy, and masculinity desires. She also contended that the masculine attitudes in women must be viewed as reaction-formations and as the result of incorrect identification. In my examination of defective identification in impulsive characters, I was constrained to share her position.[10] In his most recent work Freud does not maintain that his explanation of female object selection is generally valid *(op. cit.)*. On the other hand, one would gather from the work of H. Deutsch that penis envy provides the original motor force behind all important female attitudes (the child as a penis substitute, female sexual pleasure in coitus as the result of identification with the male). It is certainly impossible to

[9] "Zur Genese des weiblichen Kastrationskomplexes," *Internationale Zeitschrift für Psychoanalyse*, X, 1924.

[10] The chapter on defective identification in "Der triebhafte Charakter," *Neue Arbeiten zur Ärztlichen Psychoanalyse*, Nr. IV, 1925 ["The Impulsive Character," in *Early Writings*, Vol I (New York: Farrar, Straus and Giroux, 1975)].

reach a generally valid conclusion on the question of which develops first, the desire for a child and female passivity or penis desire and masculine aggressiveness. However, if one also differentiates between drive goal and drive object in the question of female sexuality, it is possible to remove some seeming contradictions that further obstruct clarification of the problem.

The fact that vaginal organization, which later becomes the basis of affirmed femininity, does not exist in childhood speaks for the views of Freud and H. Deutsch. They maintain that clitoral masturbation during the Oedipal stage and puberty is a typical finding and that penis desire is always present, even if it does not play a primarily pathological role in all cases; it may be found, for example, in the most feminine and motherly of women (as was emphasized by Horney [*op. cit.*]). Accordingly, "penis desire" and "masculinity desire" are not identical. The latter never occurs without the former, but the reverse is not true. The masculinity complex in women is the characterological expression of penis desire and can develop only if identification with a man (the father) has occurred in the ego. This is usually the case in female compulsion neurotics. In female hysterics, on the other hand, penis desire usually exerts no substantial influence on feminine and motherly attitudes and expresses itself in isolated cases as a specific symptom. Analysis of the development of heterosexual object love in the various types of frigid women reveals that this development depends less on clitoral eroticism and penis desire than on the external conditions to which identification is subjected.

In some women who reject men and heterosexuality and also exhibit a pronounced masculine bearing, the father's behavior has led to early and total identification with him.

They received too little love and kindness from the father, who was most often strict, aloof, cold, and occasionally even brutal. In their sadistic fantasies such women appear with these same traits, which are in peculiar contrast to their scorn for "brutal men." When the positive transference of such women intensifies in analysis, desires for a child, which correspond to an earlier stage of libido development, emerge from the deeper strata of the unconscious, together with tendencies toward female submission to the analyst (father). When the analysis of such cases was pursued back to the limits of memory, it was found that the primal scene had been experienced in total mother identification. It was also possible to discover the age at which father identification occurred, superimposing itself on mother identification and excluding it from participation in character formation. For example, in the patient suffering from vasomotor neurosis reported in Chapter 4 the primal scene played an important role in the creation of father identification in that the father's brutal behavior coincided completely with the "wrestling scene" the little girl heard at night. Thus, she necessarily arrived at the conclusion that the mother was being beaten, injured, or castrated. The Oedipal attitude ended with aversion toward the father which, in turn, resulted in the cessation of mother identification and the introjection of the relinquished father. Since the girl identified with the mother in the primal scene, castration fear was the only possible motive for turning away from the father.

This was also illustrated through positive reactions to therapy by similar patients. Once positive transference had aroused their maternal identification, masochistically colored coitus fantasies began to appear in daydreams and at night. At first they were warded off by an acute intensification of masculinity and hatred of men. Since the deepest motive for this resistance was, clearly, genital anxiety, these women could no longer endure intercourse, whereas they had tolerated it previously. With or without the affect of anxiety, they now felt that something might happen to them.

This fear of the loss of the penis is not difficult to understand: the belief that one possesses something gives rise to the fear of losing it, and in these cases, after father identification had been established, the *desire* to possess a penis was, in fact, transformed into an unconscious fantasy of actually having one (one patient with this fantasy always urinated standing over the toilet bowl). Comprehension of castration fear before the formation of father identification is more difficult, since only the desire for a penis exists at that time. This, indeed, excludes castration anxiety in the strict sense. However, because they believe that the clitoris will grow, and have already experienced pleasure from it, many girls fear further injury to this already mutilated genital. Nevertheless, in reference to women, the term "genital anxiety" is better suited to the psychological facts than "castration anxiety."

In the case of vasomotor neurosis cited above, the father identification, which creates the characterological masculinity complex, was thus a result of the denial that the girl experienced through her father, not of penis desire (at least not directly). The latter had existed at first by itself, independent of mother identification, and conflicted with mother identification only when confronted by the father's denials. It was solely through father identification, the result entirely of externally caused experiences, that penis desire received the force we later see operating in the character and symptoms.

That penis desire does not always lead to masculinity may be verified by comparing the patients described above with others who always exhibited feminine and even maternal traits (despite hysteria), traits based on mother identification in the ego. The pubertal "activity thrust" described by H. Deutsch *(op. cit.)* was a transient phenomenon[11] and incapable of effecting any noteworthy change in the basic feminine characteristics of the personality.

Analysis of the development of object relationships in such cases demonstrates the great influence that the actual behavior and character of the father exert on the development and preservation of femininity. Let us assume that the father shows the daughter a great deal of restrained love, although he himself is not feminine or under the domination of the mother. Inner denial is thus not augmented by any such gross external rejections as those described previously, and there is no particular reason for total father identification. Mother identification can also continue to exist because object love is satisfied at least in its tender aspect. All that is lacking for complete confirmation of that identification is a vaginal erotic basis, which cannot develop due to neurotic conflicts. Among these conflicts, shyness about her incestuous desire and guilt feelings toward the mother play the most important role, in contrast to the type first described, where heterosexual sensuality is stifled by genital anxiety. In serious cases of hysteria, we naturally see, in addition, severe coitus anxiety (genital anxiety).

There are also differences between these two types of frigidity in terms of clitoral masturbation. Comparison

[11] However, the activity thrust cannot be said to be a typical precursor of feminine passivity. I treated one patient with chronic depression and a masculine character in whom I was able to ascertain the opposite process. At the time of her first menstruation, feminine submission fantasies toward the father had emerged. She was thoroughly frightened when she noticed that she now experienced his kisses differently than before. She withdrew and was pronouncedly masculine from then on.

shows that in the compulsion neurotic, masculine type, clitoral masturbation is accompanied by sadistic and active homosexual fantasies, whereas in the hysteric-feminine type it is accompanied by heterosexual and very frequently masochistic coitus ideas.

These facts explain the seeming differences between the views of Freud and H. Deutsch on the one hand, and of Horney and myself on the other. The former are talking about the phallic-masculine libido, which, they maintain, develops first; we are referring to the little girl's psychic attitude toward her father, which, we believe, develops first and is the preliminary stage of the later feminine attitude. The fact that little girls initially desire their fathers at a time when they themselves believe that they have a masculine organ (coitus fantasy with clitoral orgasm) complicates female sexual development. For the moment there is nothing to contradict the concept that female organ libido is originally masculine, whereas the female psychic attitude (with one exception[12]) is normally always feminine, or is at least similar to the femininity that develops later.

Whether a girl discovers the penis of a playmate or a sibling before or after she acquires the desire for a child through, say, a birth being brought to her attention may be entirely a matter of chance. And it is highly questionable whether a comparison of genitalia *before* the genital phase affects the castration complex; certainly the prerequisite for this complex is the discovery and narcissistic cathexis of the genitalia as a source of pleasure. More important is the fact that penis desire and the desire

[12] If, from the beginning, a brutal father prevents a girl from developing her mother identification, the result is either permanent fixation on the mother and later a completely infantile personality, or identification with the father even before she can learn to love him. This condition was found in impulsive masochistic psychopaths with severe infantilism.

for a child, the two extremes, coexist peacefully until, during the stormy Oedipal period, highly individual and diverse fates cause penis and child to be equated, in one direction or the other. The girl then emerges from the Oedipus conflict either with a masculinity complex or a mother identification. The already activated clitoral eroticism plays no particular role in this.

If the girl's Oedipal phase concludes characterologically with mother identification, this identification can be compatible with clitoral eroticism only until puberty, when, following the reawakening of old conflicts, it will finally give way to a masculinity complex if it is not placed on a basis of vaginal primacy.

The question of how vaginal primacy develops remains essentially unanswered. In his *Three Contributions to the Theory of Sex* Freud expressed the opinion that clitoral eroticism is normally shifted to the vagina during puberty. However, he did not comment in detail on the nature and conditions under which this process takes place. Comparative studies have shown that the most important precondition for the change is mother identification in the ego. Yet despite the presence of this psychic attitude, we must inquire how "phallic clitoral" eroticism is capable of "transforming itself" into receptive vaginal eroticism, because a mere shift without such a transformation would be difficult to imagine.

I believe it was Jekels[13] who first postulated a causal relationship between anality and vaginal eroticism due to the receptive quality (cavity) they have in common. Ferenczi[14] and Lou Andreas-Salomé later advocated the same view. Recently, H. Deutsch found that in addition to anal qualities, the vagina also assumes oral qualities

[13] "Einige Bemerkungen zur Triebtheorie," *Internationale Zeitschrift für Psychoanalyse*, I, 1913.
[14] "Versuch einer Genitaltheorie," *Internationale Psychoanalytische Bibliothek*, Bd. XV.

(again, receptive). The sucking action of the vagina is even phenomenologically ascertainable. In my examination of the development of the female super-ego (*op. cit.*) I reached the conclusion that the "mother identification in the ego" is based upon anal and oral qualities and that "after the phallic denial, a partial regression to earlier stages of libido development is part of normal development in women." Study of female orgasm disturbances not only yielded further proof of the views cited but also forced me to the conclusion that only the shift of anal and oral libido to the vagina makes possible the indispensable "transformation" of clitoral eroticism, the keystone in the establishment of vaginal primacy. These transformations involve only a shift in psychic-libidinal interest, not a physiological process. The vagina has its own physiological erogeneity, which is unable to emerge as long as the clitoris, with its strong psychic cathexis and physiological erogeneity, obstructs the way. However, once oral-receptive and anal-passive libidinal interest has taken possession of the vagina (through mother identification), the clitoris becomes more or less uninteresting psychically. This does not entail a loss of physiological excitability; on the contrary, the clitoris now has an important role in foreplay and in coitus. However, interest in the excitation of this organ decreases as soon as the new pleasure source, the vagina, has been discovered, because the latter can now satisfy all libidinal demands, corresponds to the biological sexual role, and, in contrast to clitoral eroticism, creates no psychic conflicts.

In conclusion, we must differentiate three basic elements in the concept of genitality:

1. The *local erogeneity of the genital zone* (genital excitability).

2. The *psychogenital libido* (genital desire).
3. The *somatic libido* centered in the genitals (genital urgency).

All three are closely interrelated, although each has a different basis. Genital erogeneity is based on the specific irritability of the genital nerve endings, which have the quality of intense sensuality. Psychogenital libido, as a special state of psychosexual energy, may be traced to genital erogeneity, and expresses by its very nature a turning of the psychosexual interest toward the genital zone. Somatic libido, general physical sexual excitation, originates in the vegetative nervous system; its source lies in endocrine processes (in hypothetical sexual chemistry). *The orgasm (and with it the regulation of sexual economy) is ensured only if well-developed psychogenital impulses can, without disturbance, concentrate somatic sexual excitation in the genital zone.* The reason that only the genital apparatus is able to provide an orgasm must lie in the physiological structure of the various erogenous zones.

A disturbance in any one of these three elements of genitality causes orgastic impotence and somatic sexual stasis, as when, for example, perception of genital stimulation is repressed, or psychic genital libido is transferred to another erogenous zone, or pregenital libido takes possession of the genitals because psychogenitality is insufficiently developed. In all such cases, the course of somatic sexual excitation suffers.

Among the numerous expressions of dammed-up libido (stasis anxiety, conversion symptoms, compulsion symptoms), the intensification of the destructive drive is one to which little attention has heretofore been given. It is this issue that we shall now discuss.

CHAPTER SEVEN

Sexual Stasis, Aggression, Destruction, and Sadism

The intensity of those destructive impulses that lack reality-based motivations, particularly brutality and sadism, depends on the immediate degree of sexual stasis. This dependence can be observed physically as well as in psychic attitudes. Actually, psychic attitudes and physical excitations cannot be separated. Even in acute neurasthenia resulting from incomplete satisfaction and maintained by sexual stasis, an increase in destructive impulses is observable in the form of irritability, eruptions of anger over trivialities, and severe motor restlessness. Destructive impulses are identical with muscular motor tension. Unless dammed-up sexual excitation is bound in symptoms or expressed as stasis anxiety, it seizes the muscular apparatus, manifesting itself as a destructive impulse rather than a sexual phenomenon.

Motor unrest, impulses to destroy, or at least to use the muscular apparatus, as well as the general aggressiveness in sadistic-impulsive characters, become increasingly intense the longer a patient lives in abstinence. These impulses decrease when abstinence is renounced for even a

169

short period. Motor unrest expressed as an impulse to roam or as fugue states corresponding to the unconscious search for a sexual object and sexual satisfaction, is also based on sexual excitation transferred to the musculature.

Infants begin to bite when they are weaned. The leap that excitation takes from the realm of erotic sensitivity to that of motor destructiveness is also observable in children who are in the process of suppressing masturbation. It is not by chance that motor agility, cruelty, and the pleasure derived from violent motion increase so greatly at approximately the age of five.

Between the beginning and the end of puberty the character normally changes. In the beginning, dreaminess, sentimentality, and an inclination to a universal love of mankind predominate. Later, when the struggle against masturbation begins, the character tends toward loutishness, mischievousness, spite, prankishness with parents and teachers, pugnaciousness, and strenuous activity in sports. One is reminded of high-school days, when the seventh- and eighth-graders (ninth-graders less frequently) were the bane of the teachers' lives.

In other areas, too, we see that unrelieved sexual excitation is easily transformed into aggressiveness and even brutality, just as disappointed love easily turns into hate. During menstruation, and especially shortly before it begins, neurotic women tend to be highly irritable, aggressive, or depressed. With my female psychopathic patients, who were, without exception, frigid, I was able to infer the start of their periods from the increase in their aggressiveness. Psychiatry views ill temper during menstruation as a direct consequence of the somatic menstrual process and, accordingly, attempts to influence it through organic therapy. However, irritability and aggressiveness are psychic reactions to genital bleeding. Most women feel at a disadvantage in relation to men because of menstruation; their depression corresponds to the repression of destructive tendencies. This reaction is not purely psychic; in many cases aggression and sadistic fantasies intensify even before the woman realizes that her menstruation is about to begin. This is usually true in neurotic women, due to the irregularity of their periods. When such women achieve orgastic potency, or even genital sensitivity, the ill temper yields to local and general sexual excitation that corresponds to the normal heightening of sexual excitation shortly before and during menstruation. Women who have been cured of their frigidity no longer suffer from the sexual stasis that either increases aggressiveness or is expressed as stasis anxiety. Expectation of sexual satisfaction no longer produces hate or fear as it did when it was repressed. On the contrary, it heightens the readiness for love.

Castrated animals (capons, oxen, dogs, etc.) are not at all aggressive, as opposed to stallions and bulls, which become more aggressive the more rarely they are permitted to mate. After mating, aggression as well as sexual tension wanes. When watchdogs are to be made especially vicious, they are chained and kept away from bitches in heat. The phlegmatic disposition of eunuchs who were castrated before puberty also demonstrates that sexual stasis is an important source of energy for aggression. Married people who torment and physically abuse each other are usually suffering from a lack of sexual satisfaction.

In the beginning of the climacteric, people rebel against growing old by increasing their sexual activity. The less they were satisfied in the course of their lives, the more pronounced their rebellion will be. Not infrequently, impulses of sexual cruelty also surface during the climacteric.

That the destructive drive is indeed dependent on the

state of sexual tension is further demonstrated by the fact that aggressive and cruel inclinations disappear spontaneously after a satisfying sexual act. Genital orgasm clearly withdraws the destructive energies from the muscular system.

In contrast to drive-inhibited individuals, persons who later develop uninhibited sadistic tendencies have experienced uninhibited sexual satisfaction in very early childhood. Destructive aggression was fully aroused only when sexual satisfaction was brutally suppressed by the parents or their surrogates. Ruthless denial of sexual satisfaction was felt as all the more harsh, because genitality had been fully developed and, to the extent allowed by the physiological conditions, also satisfied. Such children become incapable of loving, since hate has suffocated every loving impulse. Nevertheless, they crave love, and later their hate is strongest where they demand love the most, namely, in the parental home. They are adept at inviting disappointment: they always desire those love objects that are unattainable and always behave in such a way as to earn sharp rejection. Both their sensual desires and their reaction to the inevitable disappointments are uninhibited, impulsive. In addition, their reactions are markedly sadistic, that is, aggressive-destructive in the sexual sense. The denied sexual impulse is clearly manifest in the nature of the aggression and in the object toward which it is directed. Thus, denial of sexual satisfaction has caused destructive aggression to emerge; the impulses of revenge have transmuted the sexual drive demand that was denied into a tendency toward destructiveness and sadism.

Ample proof for this interpretation of the emergence of sadism may also be found in the domain of drive-inhibited compulsion neurosis and hysteria. I would remind the reader of the way the compulsive woman [Chapter 5, pp. 120 ff] reacted to her emerging love tendency: she hated the object of her desire because she did not allow herself to perceive her feelings of love and feared him as she feared all other love objects. At the same time, her sadistic fantasies, with their unmistakable sexual character, increased inordinately. The processes that in this case took place unconsciously are overt in impulsive individuals, who inconsiderately demand declarations of love, and when in treatment may even threaten to poison the physician who rejects them. However, they never give rejection as a motive for these murderous intentions. Their easily injured pride and their guilt feelings prohibit this, so they find an irrelevant rationalization, or simply declare that murder, castration, or arson would certainly make them well; that they can find total satisfaction only in such activities; or that they merely need, just once, to give full vent to their emotions.

The relationship of the destructive drive to neurotic anxiety is not as simple as its relationship to sexual stasis. In the past, Adler denied the libidinal source of neurotic anxiety and maintained that it is a reaction to aggressive impulses. From a superficial perspective, this theory is correct. When impulsive characters restrain their sadistic impulses, anxiety is aroused; however, it does not disappear when the impulses are acted upon, as does stasis anxiety after sexual satisfaction. On the contrary, it intensifies. The social meaning of "aggression anxiety" could also account for the qualitative difference between it and libidinal anxiety, but this cannot be correct because our research has proven clinically that the intensity of sadism is dependent on sexual stasis. We might also add that aggressive psychopathic females develop the most severe moral anxiety or aggression anxiety during menstruation, whether or not they actually become aggressive.

What is the genetic difference between sexual anxiety and aggression (or moral) anxiety? The ego reacts to the drive restrictions of the external world with anxiety. If these restrictions are not obeyed, punishment can be expected (e.g., castration as punishment for masturbation). Therefore, since the ego is incapable of mastering its drive demands, it is forced to repress them. However, the fear of being punished does not disappear but continues to exist as guilt, because the feared punisher becomes internalized in the ego, as an ingrained "thou shalt not." The term "moral anxiety" accounts fully for guilt feelings originating in fear of punishment. Guilt *is* moral anxiety; it is merely a superstructure built on castration anxiety, which, in turn, acts as the model for all fear of punishment (Freud). People believe themselves to be profoundly moral when they are, essentially, merely afraid, as may be seen in the analysis of every compulsion neurotic.

However, if we examine the nature of guilt feelings and moral anxiety more carefully and compare these to the infantile fear of punishment, we shall see an essential difference. Castration anxiety is the immediate ego reaction to the perception of a prohibited sexual drive demand. Moral anxiety, on the other hand, is primarily a reaction to the perception of a repressed destructive-sadistic tendency and must therefore be termed aggression anxiety. It signifies the individual's fear of being destroyed if he behaves in a selfish, cruel, or antisocial manner, whereas genital anxiety signifies the individual's neurotic fear of genital injury if he submits to a sexual drive impulse.

Thus, in order to transform genital anxiety into guilt, there must be something to supplement it. This supplement consists of an aggressive-destructive reaction to the danger of castration (or to a denial of sexual satisfaction). The process, most clearly observable in compulsion neurosis, is as follows: The child is denied satisfaction of a sexual impulse; he reacts to this in part with castration anxiety and in part with aggressive feelings toward the individual who inflicted the denial on him. Hate is, after all, the natural reaction to denial or restriction of a striving for pleasure. Death wishes (and in extreme cases impulses to murder) accompany this hate; but since the hated object is also loved, there develops a fear of acting on the murderous impulse against the loved object. This aggression anxiety then combines with castration anxiety, since one must risk one's own castration if one wishes to rob the father of his penis. Thus, moral anxiety (aggression anxiety) is indeed the direct expression of an inhibited impulse of revenge, although it cannot develop solely from a hate-revenge situation. Pure hate leads to action without guilt. It is love for the object, as well as for oneself, that causes moral anxiety.

Although guilt feelings, too, are evoked by inhibited or repressed aggression, it must not be overlooked that aggression itself is essentially a reaction to the denial of pleasure; that is to say, in the depths of the mechanisms that produce guilt feelings, sexual conflicts are always at work.

Hence we see the same dynamic in both situations. Hate depends upon the intensity of the love denied, the destructive drive, upon the intensity of sexual stasis. Even healthy individuals are subject to aggression anxiety, but in them it appears merely as an unemotional moral inhibition without sexual stasis. It is only the presence of sexual stasis that explains why in neurotics moral anxiety may emerge with all the characteristics of affective anxiety. Sexual stasis, the actual source of all neurotic phenomena, is the basis of all these complicated psychic reactions.

Let us now summarize the distinctions between aggression, destruction, and sadism:

Aggression is every kind of *active* achievement, be it capturing a sexual partner, mastering a problem, or overcoming difficulties of daily life. Aggression is part of normal healthy behavior in all activities undertaken vis-à-vis the world.

Destruction is the eradication of dangerous objects or impediments. It is biologically based behavior and can be rational as well as irrational or neurotic. It is always the latter when dictated by unconscious and repressed motives and contents.

Sadism is always ultimately destructive and cruel. Arising from dammed-up sexual excitation, its purpose is sexual gratification. In this sense, sadism is always pathological, a sure sign of a disturbed sexual economy, wherever and whatever the context. (*Masochism*, according to sex-economic investigations, is not the opposite of sadism; that is, it is not the expression of a striving for pleasure through pain [as is claimed by psychoanalysis]. Masochism, whether erotic or moral, is an act of aggression against the other person, an act that makes use of suffering as its means. Physiologically it corresponds to the drive for guiltless release of tension, or satisfaction, through the other person. However, masochism is not a drive in the biological sense. It does not exist in the animal world any more than does sadism. Both are symptoms of social pathology.)

CHAPTER EIGHT

The Social Significance
of
Genital Strivings

In the preceding chapter we established that aggressive attitudes toward the world increase when genital strivings meet with internal or external obstacles. In compulsion neurosis the penis becomes a fantasized instrument of hate, and genital eroticism is enlisted in the service of the destructive drive. We found that genital satisfaction relieves destructiveness, that a lack or deficiency of satisfaction precipitates it, and that a removal of the source of sexual impulses causes destructiveness to become permanently inactive. We were able to confirm this with examples from the animal kingdom.

If suppression of genitality—particularly of genital satisfaction—intensifies sadistic impulses, we must assume that the general cultural negation of sexuality and the tendency to fragment and suppress it has played a decisive role in the emergence of human sadism.

The Fragmenting of Genital
Tendencies in Society

In animals the destructive drive appears exclusively as an oral killing instinct, which subserves either self-preservation or self-defense. Carnivorous beasts of prey kill suitable objects when hunger requires. Captive predatory animals are not dangerous when their hunger is completely satisfied. Their aggressiveness toward strangers is caused by an instinctive sense of danger, as is proven by their quite contrary behavior toward their trainer. Nothing similar to the phallic and anal sadism of humans, such as stabbing, shooting, drilling through, beating, squashing, trampling, exists here.[1]

The human destructive drive is distinguished primarily by the fact that its goals are not biological necessities. (In this respect it is just like the ferocity of some animals when they are unable to achieve sexual satisfaction.) Its future destiny is decisively influenced by the social environment and the individual's ability to adjust to it. At its extremes the destructive drive can emerge either bearing asocial, cruel characteristics (as in cases of sexual homicide) or as compulsive hypermorality, which betrays its origins through its intolerance and austerity. Let us recall, for instance, the austerity of Catholic dogma and especially the cruelty of the Inquisition, which accompanied religious hypermorality and pretended to protect it. The religious demand for and observance of asceticism itself resulted from deep-seated guilt feelings; the original sin in the myth of Adam and Eve was a genital act forbidden by God the Father. The external denial developed into an in-

---

[1] The genital aggression used to overcome the female cannot be termed sadism.

ternal prohibition, exactly as in compulsion neurosis. Furthermore, Freud and Reik[2] have proven that religious ceremonies obey exactly the same laws as compulsion-neurotic ceremonials. However, to the best of my knowledge, the fact that it was suppression of genital impulses which produced brutality has not yet been given due recognition. Sadism developed first and was subsequently perverted to religious masochism. Thus, medieval masochistic orgies and the excessive brutality of the Inquisition were essentially discharge manifestations of libidinal energies. De Coster, who brilliantly described the Inquisition, portrayed these facts in the figures of Philip II and Till Eulenspiegel. In contrast to the neurotic and cruel Philip, Till Eulenspiegel, the Protestant who scorns and negates the principle of asceticism, appears as a model of a basically benevolent individual. Further, he is a symbol of the salutary influence the aboliton of ascetic principles exerted on Protestantism. He was at odds with Catholicism, at least in the beginning, through his tolerance and kindness.

Let us now shift our attention to an examination of current sexual morality as represented by traditional, capitalist middle-class society. Here we are struck by elements that are fully analogous to compulsion-neurotic ideology:

1. Extramarital sexual intercourse is generally portrayed as animalistic (sadistic) and dirty (anal).
2. With no consideration for physiological and biological facts, premarital and extramarital asceticism is promulgated often by physicians.
3. Masturbation is viewed as the evil of evils, even by physicians, although it is factually irrefutable that

[2] "Beiträge zur Religionspsychologie," *Internationale Psychoanalytische Bibliothek*, Bd. V, 1921.

masturbation normally dominates a certain phase
of development.

4. Love impulses are fragmented: young, unmarried
men are allowed intercourse, but since the girls of
the same class are to be protected, prostitution is
tolerated as a "filthy" but necessary evil.

The concept of sexual intercourse as an animalistic and
dirty matter causes it to be judged not as a biological,
physiological, and psychic necessity but as an evacuation
process similar to defecation. The sensual component of
genitality is separated from the tender; young men satisfy
their sensuality in an "affair" with a girl whom they
would never accept as a wife precisely because she gave
herself without a marriage license, or they resort to prostitutes while simultaneously "idolizing" a girl of their own
class. The greater this idolization, the more indignantly
they reject the thought of an intimate relationship with
her; and if the girl were to yield to their sensual demands,
they would lose their tender impulses toward her. As an
exalted woman, the girl unconsciously represents the
mother, whom the son must not suspect of sexuality,
since it was she who prohibited as obscene the pleasurable
autoerotic activities. However, while exalting the female,
many neurotics simultaneously manifest a deep contempt
for women. One of the motives for this is the bitter,
unavoidable disappointment that children experience.
They become aware that their parents, the mother in
particular, engage in activities similar to those which
were forbidden to them. The entire situation is repressed,
and there remains only doubt of both divine and human justice, extreme overvaluation or undervaluation of
women, compulsive religiosity or forced atheism, and last
but not least, the inability to unite sensual and tender im-

pulses. Only half of the personality can participate in the sexual experience. This always entails a reduction in psychogenital satisfaction, with all its consequences. Of these, the increase in sadistic-aggressive impulses is unquestionably the most socially significant.

Apart from the irrational motives that are reproduced in the double sexual standard, social motives play a decisive role in shaping the differing views on female and male extramarital sexual intercourse (including "adultery"). Socioeconomic interests determine morality, which in turn manifests itself in the individual as a personal opinion about sexuality. Secondarily these moral judgments acquire a justification in the uncivilized and unnatural relationship actually existing between the sexes in bourgeois society. Prevailing sexual morality first debases sexual feelings, particularly in the sexual act, and then refers to the baseness it itself has created, declaring sexual needs to be unnatural and harmful to health.[3] As a result a woman's involvement in an extramarital love affair is appraised differently than a man's, even by those without prejudice. This fact is expressed in common speech: the woman has "thrown herself away," whereas the man has "possessed the woman"—and the reverse is never the case. This is because, for the majority of men, "possessing" a woman signifies a conquest; furthermore, possessing a married woman represents a triumph over the "betrayed" husband. The primary issue is therefore not the sexual experience but "possession," "loss," "betrayal," "triumph,"

---

[3] This sexual morality, although rooted in the views and interests of the economically well-to-do and the aristocracy, reaches far beyond these circles and thrives especially in those of minor civil servants, employees, and the petite bourgeoisie. Nor is the urban proletariat free of it, and one can observe that proletarians adopt bourgeois sexual morality to the extent that their life style assimilates that of the petite bourgeoisie. *Cf.* in this connection "Sexual Maturity, Continence, Marital Morality" (1930) [in *The Sexual Revolution* (New York: Farrar, Straus and Giroux, 1969)].

"revenge." Thus, it is inconceivable in bourgeois sensibility for a husband who feels temporarily involved else-
where to tell his wife candidly.

Obviously, under such circumstances the orgastic experience must give way to the joys of conquest, betrayal,
secretiveness, and "desertion." Middle-class morality
weakens orgastic potency and this, in turn, distorts genital
object love and confirms the double sexual standard. For
orgastically potent individuals, coitus is neither proof of
potency, nor a conquest, nor an act of revenge toward a
third party. It is, rather, a necessary, pleasurable experience, without ulterior motive. This applies to women
just as to men. The non-frigid woman has ceased to be a
mere sexual tool: she "takes" just as much as she "gives,"
exactly as the man does. It is absolutely clear that affirmation of genitality counteracts the debasement of sexual
life.

The factor that, with good reason, reinforces the
bourgeois in his views on sexual matters is the sexual
prurience of the average middle-class male and of the sexually inhibited middle-class female who have been raised
under false principles. This prurience is itself a result of
strong natural sexual desire and bourgeois sexual morality,
which imbues natural sexual relationships with a damaging quality of coarseness by depicting the sexual act as
something unclean or animalistic.

This sociopsychological situation is complicated by a
remarkable fact: regardless of how aggressive and eman-
cipated they are beforehand, women become enslaved to
men who bring them to orgasm. After a satisfying sexual
experience, they want this strong, controlling man. In less
intelligent women a strange wish for dependence and
subordination even emerges. Healthy men, on the other
hand, are protected from dependency by the phallic-

aggressive character of their sexuality. Only an unsatisfied or feminine man can become sexually dependent on a woman, for which dependence she secretly despises him.

In our day, however, it is hard to decide whether this inclination to sexual enslavement on the part of women is the result of their sexual education in the bourgeois world or of psychosexual characteristics. Equally valid arguments could be adduced for either assumption. One thing is certain: out of the biological relation of the sexes, prevailing sexual codes and morality have created a craving for power in men and, in reaction, a masculinization of women—and orgastic impotence in both sexes. Unquestionably, the natural female reaction to the lack of a penis is very significantly, perhaps even decisively, intensified by the disparagement of women that is fostered by the double sexual standard. Little girls are constantly being told that they cannot do, or may not do, as much as boys. Thus, a continuous cycle of effects is established: the unsublimated pride of penis of the average bourgeois man leads to the disparagement of women; this, in turn, makes women masculine, sexually timid, and frigid. Their frigidity detracts from their value as an object of sexual desire, because women who are emotionally cold during intercourse arouse in the man the feeling of having before him merely a tool of satisfaction. This feeling strengthens anew male arrogance and the contempt for women.

The idea that women "suffer" the act, that it involves something degrading for them, cannot be explained solely by the "sadistic concept of coitus" because, first, this concept implies that the woman does something to the man during the act; second, the idea of intercourse as a burden to women exists among people whose attitude toward the sexual act is not sadistic. It is more likely that this view developed from the general debasement of love life that

has come about since the establishment of private owner-
ship of the means of production, and from the sadistic-
derogatory attitude of men toward women.

The Consequences for Marriage of
the Fragmenting of Sexuality

A feature that is important in the premarital sex life of
men plays a disastrous role in marriage. As is known, prostitutes are either totally frigid or are orgastically potent
only with their lovers, the "pimps." Younger prostitutes
occasionally simulate an orgasm, but this act soon ceases
to impress an experienced man and may even cause
disgust. Before long, the man becomes apathetic toward
the woman, and the sexual act sinks to the level of an
autoerotic, masturbational act, inspired no longer by a
woman but by fantasies only. The general attitude toward
women that this creates is best characterized by expressions frequently heard among officers and students: "a
hole is a hole," "they're all the same in the dark," and
many others of the sort. Some men seek compensation for
the lack of shared pleasure by engaging in diverse coital
variations which, under such circumstances, yield little
satisfaction.

It is highly significant that many men and women have
never even heard of the female orgasm; many others actually consider it disgraceful. In some men the contempt
they feel for women and the apathy engendered by "anal"
and onanistic intercourse with paid women arouse disgust
after coitus, and frequently even during ejaculation.
Later, in marriage, it is difficult for them to overcome this
reaction; genital sensuality is so burdened with anality
that it is unable to find the connection with tender im-

pulses. Intercourse with the wife who is loved tenderly, assuming that tender love can still be evoked, is viewed, consciously or unconsciously, as defiling her. If tender impulses die, intercourse becomes a bothersome chore, nothing more than a process of evacuation. If these impulses do not revive, the man is in danger of becoming facultatively or totally impotent. Naturally the wife's genitality, which she was constrained to suppress until marriage, also suffers; indeed, during the initial period of the sexual relationship, great tact and understanding on the part of the husband are required for her to overcome her sexual timidity. The husband, however, has usually not acquired an interest in satisfying a woman; and if his wife were to allow her excitement free rein, it would remind him of a prostitute's simulation of sexual passion. Thus, the social fragmenting of sexuality, revealed in the contrast between marriage and prostitution, must be viewed as one of the most significant causes for continuing frigidity in women who are otherwise not neurotically so disposed. Lack of interest in satisfying a woman causes early ejaculation and subsequent penile flaccidity; the husband strives for his own end pleasure without adjusting to his wife who, especially in the beginning of a marriage, achieves an orgasm only with difficulty, if at all. This state of affairs fosters in her a regressive revival of early fantasies, and so lays the groundwork for psychoneurosis. When treating frigid women, this socially induced form of premature ejaculation is encountered as a final but insurmountable obstacle. The woman's genitality, although liberated through analysis, cannot develop because the husband is not sufficiently potent; in other words, he has not overcome the fragmenting of his sexual impulses. He continues to behave egotistically as he did previously with prostitutes or kept women.

In other cases, men lack the opportunity in marriage to use the coital variations they practiced earlier, or to achieve extragenital satisfaction, because they cannot expect "such brothel practices" from their wives, who are much too inhibited to be active themselves; any extragenital sexuality is associated with the idea of "degenerate prostitutes." However, analysis of married women shows that, to the extent they have not been sublimated and in a degree varying with the individual, pregenital drive impulses require satisfaction in foreplay. Knowledge of sexual development in general allows us no other assumption. Accordingly, rejection of all nongenital satisfaction is based on repression. Men who suppress their unsublimated pregenital needs are also threatened with a neurosis. Such restrictions always lead to irritability in the marriage, the actual causes of which usually remain unconscious or repressed. If the husband fragments his sexuality again by satisfying his genitality in the socially permissible marital act and his pregenital impulses outside his marriage, the results may be no less damaging to the marriage.

The inhibition or fragmentation of needs causes a progressive reduction of sexual attraction; orgastic discharge progressively diminishes in intensity; fantasies stemming from unrelieved impulses arise in a disturbing fashion during the act; and, finally, aggression wells up, directed primarily against the supposedly culpable spouse. Moreover, the polygamous desires emerging in the wake of this situation cause guilt feelings in morally restrained husbands, further intensifying the hate. If the husband has no opportunity to sublimate suppressed elements through his work, or if his capacity to sublimate is slight, his homosexuality emerges, and he becomes a gambler or drinker.

If the wife has strong sexual feelings but is inhibited, her path must lead to neurosis. The disappointment she feels in her husband need not always become conscious. The stronger the repression, the more certain it is that satisfaction will be sought in fantasies, resulting inevitably in regression and a damming-up of sexual energy, or the yearning for satisfaction emerging as bitterness and conflict. The outcome will be determined by the strength of the moral inhibition. Many bad marriages are traceable to the fact that husband and wife were unable to find each other genitally. The marital battle is then nothing but a masked neurosis.

For a frigid woman, intercourse is always irksome and appears brutal. For her and her husband, who rightly relates her repulsion to himself, it becomes a burdensome duty. In such cases, not even sublimation can help, because the disruption of the sex life also undermines existing sublimations. Often an inability to work develops, leaving only the choice between neurosis and marital infidelity.

Under certain circumstances, a large family and great material need may offer an escape from such difficulties by absorbing psychic energy that would otherwise have concentrated to form a neurosis. Women to some extent are able to find in their children a substitute for deficient sexual satisfaction. However, it would be useless to attempt to completely replace sexual satisfaction with work or an abundance of children, for example, in the service of a religious or philosophical concept. Under certain conditions inherent in neurosis formation, a neurosis will develop despite poverty, external work obligations, and a large family.

Desire for a child is significantly more pronounced in women than in men. However, in the development of the individual, sexual desire always precedes the desire for a child, as can be seen in puberty. Additionally, the desire for a child can be inhibited by the denial of sexual satisfaction. Only in some neurotic women does the desire for a child occasionally shroud sexual desire. In such cases, analysis demonstrates the existence of a neurotic inhibition of genital impulses. These women unconsciously fear the sexual act or have suffered grave disappointment in men, and now desire a child parthenogenetically. Frigid women with numerous children did not originally wish to have children at all, or at least not primarily even when they are the best of mothers. Children constitute a replacement for sexual satisfaction only in the expenditure of libidinal energy their care requires. Rebellion against maternal duties and the concomitant self-denial[4] soon emerge in analysis. In relatively good marriages the desire for a child usually appears only when genital demands have achieved a certain degree of satiety.

Some people feel that a marriage is not firmly established until the birth of a child. This is true only under certain conditions. One of the most important of these is the parents' psychogenital harmony. If this does not exist, the children become a new source of marital annoyance and act as oppressive restraints from which only the very well-to-do are able to free themselves. When there are several children, all the unsatisfied marital love is poured onto them, each parent taking sides according to sex and then playing off his favorites against those of the spouse. This, of course, has very adverse effects on the children's psychic development. Such children clash severely with their parents and each other. Many a "multiple personality"—which Freud traces to contradictory, incompatible identifications—stems from such marriages.

---

[4] In "Two Women" Balzac described this maternal conflict with matchless clarity.

The Dulling of Genitality
in the Monogamous Marriage

Prevailing sexual morality requires sexual monogamy in marriage. It is not our task here to decide whether this is or is not right. Ethical postulates cannot be proved. Based as they are on value judgments, they are inaccessible to science, which merely describes and explains. Science can only weigh the postulates themselves, their social and individual motivations, and the results of adherence or nonadherence to one or another moral precept. Morality has taken many forms through the ages, making ever changing demands which have been equally defended with passion and conviction by their proponents. Despite their often emphasized amorality, scientists tend to become moralistic when touching on the issue of sexuality; this is certainly not conducive to objectivity in their findings.

Several self-evident facts must be stressed repeatedly as long as serious and influential sexologists such as Fürbinger continue to express their moral indignation in scientific tracts, as in the following, for example:

> When abnormal positions—the woman above the man, side by side, coitus *cum uxore inversa*, standing, sitting, knee-elbow position—are selected with marked frequency although no compelling reasons exist (obesity, pregnancy, gynecological ailments), doctors must avoid an inclination to view this consistently as innocent, passing impropriety[!]. Often enough this conceals subtle distortions of sensual titillation and shameless[!?] fantasy.[5]

[5] Quoted from Marcuse's *Handwörterbuch der Sexualwissenschaft*, p. 378. A note by the editors of the *Münchner Medizinische Wochenschrift* (November 1926) added to the flattering review of a book by Van der Velde, *Die Vollkommene Ehe* (Konegan Verlag, 1926, reviewed by Nassauch) demonstrates what one must expect if one voices the truth in these matters: "In our opinion it would have been better to restrict the book to physicians, as it might cause damage in

From here it is only a step to regulations specifying the "normal" coital position.

Let us disregard moral teachings and examine the facts. Years of monogamy cause a dulling of genital attraction, which only rarely ends in quiet resignation. Far more often it leads to severe marital conflict. This pivotal issue of marital sexuality has always been the subject of ribald wit and humor and has also constantly engaged great minds such as Balzac and Strindberg. Bourgeois, moralistic, timid science alone has managed to avoid the issue.

Husband and wife discover faults in each other that previously went unnoticed or overlooked. They no longer "get along" with each other, whether or not their personalities have changed. Only very rarely do they recognize the actual reasons. Usually they view their flagging sexuality as a consequence of their disharmony. Actually, the opposite is true: the decrease in sexual attraction heightens personality traits that had receded during the period of genital harmony.

Let us assume the most favorable case: a newlywed couple are physically and mentally healthy; they have been spared the stress of economic difficulties, and the husband has been able to reverse the economically and socially caused fragmenting of his love impulses. For the virgin wife, defloration is always a shock from which she can recover only under favorable circumstances. If she does not overcome her frigidity quickly, hate for her husband develops. Serious authors have claimed, and psychoanalysis of married individuals proves, that later marital happiness or unhappiness is ultimately traceable to experiences during the first sexual encounter. (Understandable but, from a medical standpoint, unjustifiable fear of

the hands of laymen. Certain 'variations' described and recommended here should not be assimilated into German marriages[!]."

acquiring the reputation of a pornographer has prevented anyone from approaching the psychology of the wedding night.) The very existence of the term "honeymoon"* to describe the first weeks of marriage implies that those who coined or enjoy using this term have already experienced the dulling of sexuality, and wish to emphasize the fictitiousness of the initial marital experiences, which appear beautiful only from the viewpoint of later dullness. In reality these first experiences have a shock effect, and are either endured with conscious disappointment or are repressed and blocked from consciousness through exaggerated, short-lived illusions. The wife confronts this new experience, tabooed from childhood, with fear; and where fear presides, there can be no pleasurable experience. The husband is also faced with a new situation. If previously he had to fragment his love impulses, he must now muster a great deal of tact and sensitivity to adjust his sensuality to the situation and not act inconsiderately. Therefore, a harmonious, pleasurable experience cannot take place. The reason the first experiences appear beautiful to many men lies in the novelty of the situation, namely, "possessing" a woman of their own class for the first time.

Women from lower economic and social strata must also react with fear when they enter marriage as virgins. Although men of their class may not have undergone a division of love impulses, they generally lack the refined sensuality necessary to avoid the shock of defloration.

Marriage-counseling offices should give priority to enlightening married couples regarding the difficulties of physical and mental adjustment. Physical examinations constitute only part of the task. Just the mere knowledge that genital harmony can only occur when the sexual

---

* *Flitterwochen* (*Flitter*, "spangle," "tinsel," "tawdry finery"; -*wochen*, "weeks"). [Trans.]

rhythms of both persons adjust to one another could spare great disappointment. A husband should know that women are usually initially frigid and that they overcome their frigidity spontaneously, assuming they are essentially healthy and their husbands are not clumsy. Of course, only psychoanalysis would probably be able to remove the difficulties in neurotic women. Now that there are psychoanalytic day clinics for the poor, even the most destitute can receive specialized analytic advice and treatment. The sexual needs of the proletariat must not be underestimated. In treating working-class women, one frequently hears that they have been accused of frigidity. Neither welfare doctors with their somatic prejudices nor psychologically untrained or inept marriage counselors are aware that these elementary difficulties exist in proletarian marriages.[6]

[6] Here is just one example. In *Deutsche Medizinische Wochenschrift*, Nr. 47, 1926, Schwalbe reports on the marriage-counseling office in Berlin, run by the Borough Hall in Penslau Berg (in "Gesundheitliche Beratung vor der Eheschliessung"). He states that the examinations proceeded according to a form: height, weight, chest circumference, body type, urine, menstruation, fatty tissue, musculature, mucous membranes, bone structure, sensory organs, eyes, ears, lungs, heart, blood pressure, vascular tonus, hemoglobin content, genitals. Especially stressed findings: hernia, cryptorchism, malformation. Then it is added that "a complete examination is undertaken only in appropriate cases." Anyone who tries to convince us that opinions have changed, or who presumes that questions of psychosexuality (potency, love capability, actual love conflicts) are viewed as so self-evident that they do not require attention, is advised to read a few sentences further in the report on the "Marital and Sexual Counseling Offices of the Federation for the Protection of Motherhood and Sexual Reform," which states that "in these offices, marriage counseling is not viewed as the only objective. In addition, advice is given on *all sexual questions* [my italics], although, unfortunately, not only on contraception but apparently also on abortion." This proves that our statements about the usual concept of marriage are correct; namely, that it is not supposed to be a sexual relationship, otherwise the words "in addition" would be senseless. The marriage-counseling office in Frankfurt (Prof. Raeke) also functions along the same lines: "Once a marriage has been contracted, no more counseling is provided. In this manner, the problem of birth control is completely eliminated"—for the marriage counselor! The fact that counseling only begins to achieve its actual purpose after marriage is likewise excluded.

Obviously, criticism here is unnecessary.

Let us return to the main subject. Once all obstacles have been overcome and genital harmony achieved, a new danger threatens: all-too-frequent intercourse. This has a double disadvantage: high libidinal tension is never achieved and even the slightest accumulation is discharged.[7] Under these circumstances, coitus becomes compulsive, and feelings of disgust arise. In addition, although in the sexual act the aggressive desire to conquer is partially satisfied, for many men whose primary premarital goal was the conquest of numerous women, desire for the wife dwindles when the necessity to conquer her disappears.

What is expressed here in crass outline occurs, to some extent, in most marriages. Its causes lie in the influences to which children's sexual development is subjected. The fact that anything sexual was always forbidden and, hence, especially coveted, continues to have an unconscious effect, namely, that everything forbidden, even in the nonsexual realm, acquires a hidden sexual connotation, as in kleptomania, for example. For some people the sexual value of what is forbidden increases pathologically, to the point where they cannot desire what is *not* forbidden. The more a man strives to "possess" and "conquer" in his premarital sex life, the more quickly will he become sexually blunted in his marriage. The narcissistic and sadistic components of genitality remain unsatisfied in monogamous marriages.

This difficulty is augmented by an element from the boy's early infantile sexual relationship to his mother. If the desire for the unattainable mother maintains its original intensity, the result, according to Rank, is a permanent inability to remain with one woman (Don Juan).

[7] To my knowledge, Ferenczi was the first to treat the dangers of marital "habitual sex" within the framework of a scientific paper. "Psychoanalyse von Sexualgewohnheiten," *Internationaler Psychoanalytischer Verlag*, 1925.

For such men the wife ceases to be the desired mother because possessing her has now become legitimate. (According to Freud, the prerequisite for love is that the woman belong to another man and be conquered illegally.) Only analytic dissolution of the incestuous fixation is of help in such cases.

There has been much debate over whether human nature is polygamous or monogamous, the decision in each case depending upon individual philosophy. More judicious people have left the question unanswered because an equal number of ethical arguments could be presented for either side. Viewed unsentimentally, morality has muddied this area of scientific research entirely. Otherwise, it would long ago have been obvious from the sex lives of animals, of primitive and civilized peoples, and of the young people in the proletariat and the upper bourgeoisie that the sexual drive knows nothing of either alternative. It knows only satisfaction.

Scientific observation more or less argues against innateness of lifelong love. Enduring monogamous sexual life is based either on sexual satisfaction or neurosis, that is, sexual repression and feelings of guilt. The need for various partners that is inherent in healthy sexuality is not to be construed as promiscuity. However, polygamy is neurotic when it is due to an inability to achieve satisfaction, repressed homosexuality, or incestuous fixation.

The extent to which a married man is able to control his polygamous tendencies depends upon the degree to which he has been able to free himself of Oedipal attitudes and find satisfaction with his wife. This applies equally to women, *mutatis mutandis*. It is also true for both sexes that polygamous wishes emerge less often the better the husband and wife recognize and satisfy each other's sensual needs and the more understanding each brings to the polygamous tendencies of the partner.

Polygamous tendencies are always aroused when important libidinal demands are not satisfied. The dulling of monogamously satisfied genitality aside, however, a significant difference may be seen between the motives of male and female polygamy. There are many women who harbor polygamous desires out of female inferiority feelings that create a need to be admired and conquered by a number of men. However, this narcissistic element may also be explained by the rejection little girls suffer from their fathers. The object-oriented type of polygamy (seeking the unattainable) may also, through severe reaction-formation, develop into the narcissistic type. The fact that more women than men belong in this category is traceable to the anatomical basis of female inferiority feelings, namely, the lack of a penis. In the narcissistic type of polygamy, as opposed to the object-oriented type, revenge tendencies, augmented by a desire to dominate the sexual object, play a considerable role. Genitally satisfied women are usually little inclined to polygamy, whereas vaginal anesthetics with pronounced clitoral eroticism generally show a lack of constancy.

Any tendency that cannot be sublimated and remains unsatisfied in marital intercourse results in genital dulling and partial estrangement from the partner, especially when it is homosexual tendencies that are involved. (I am referring here not to the neurotic form of homosexuality but rather to the physiological homosexual component in bisexuality.) When polygamous tendencies become compulsive in a marriage, one may assume, on the basis of analytic experience, that homosexual urges could not be accommodated in the marital relationship. One is led to this conclusion by the fact that men in this situation usually desire polygamous or homosexual women rather than another monogamous woman. They search for Weininger's prostitute type. In women, this occasionally emerges even more distinctly in the form of attraction to homosexual women.

If the "normal" manner of cohabitation is permanently adhered to, if every change is taboo, or if partial drives are not satisfied during foreplay, genital impulses wane very soon, or, to put it more accurately, they come into competition with the unsatisfied needs. In such cases, neurotic inhibition and repression of pregenital instinctual urges, as well as of homosexuality, are always present. A certain broad, individually varied freedom in the mode of coitus can prevent this fatal rivalry and, furthermore, minimize many forms of apathy.

In the analysis of frigid women, one discovers that their fantasies, or their preference for lying on top of the man in intercourse, correspond to a desire to be a man. Likewise, men with a strong feminine component fantasize lying beneath the woman, although if these men are neurotic, they reject this wish as being improper and feminine, sometimes with pathological consequences. However, these impulses are present in both the most masculine of men and the most feminine of women. A reversal of position (coitus inversus) is therefore at least partially able to satisfy such wishes and thus render them harmless. Coitus *a tergo* readily satisfies active male homosexuality, and for women may satisfy very early wishes stemming from an anal conception of intercourse or from early childhood observation of animals.

Many people who found pleasure in masturbation during childhood need some manual touching of their genitalia in foreplay. Some women are able to achieve orgasm only if they have been manually stimulated before intromission.[8]

One must not forget that the pregenital systems always accompany genital primacy in varying degrees of intensity (Freud). They intrude, and if they are not satisfied, press for exclusive satisfaction as perversions. Thus, for example, pronounced oral impulses will seek satisfaction exclusively in fellatio or cunnilingus.

The sexual act itself is capable of satisfying the various psychosexual demands if insistent infantile sexual impulses have not been unduly affected by repression and are allowed, to the extent they have not been sublimated or characterologically processed, to join in the flow of present sexual experience. Male and female behavior before and after satisfying intercourse proves that all desires have been fulfilled. Before intercourse the man is simultaneously tender and phallic-aggressive; the woman usually passive, awaiting the man's genital aggression. During the act her behavior changes; she, too, becomes active, until her orgasm finally coincides with the man's. Men do not achieve complete satisfaction when women are frigid or anesthetic. (Even when men have intercourse with prostitutes, they sometimes demand that their partner at least pretend to "come" with them.) Unquestionably, this implies intense participation in the partner's orgasm, a total identification that supplements one's own experience. This identification is capable of satisfying the feminine tendencies in men as well as the masculine tendencies in women.

Following satisfying intercourse, behavior is usually reversed: the woman brings all her tender, maternal qualities to bear and the man becomes like a child.

---

[8] We cannot share Kehrer's opinion that manual stimulation is harmful. If the woman falls ill, this is due only to fear of masturbation, and would have happened in any case.

Awareness of the possibility that she might have just conceived a child causes the woman to anticipate the child in the man and thus support his infantile manner. Whereas the woman's behavior was at first childlike and passive and then maternal and active, the man's is just the opposite, that is, at first fatherly and aggressive and then childlike and passive.

The difficulties and causes of the dulling of sexuality in monogamous relations that I have described cannot be eliminated, although, in principle, they may be avoided to the extent the individuals involved refuse to pay for the exercise of their moral principles with a neurosis or its equivalent, an unhappy marriage. Nevertheless, a further cause of waning interest may be permanent: libido is as inconstant as it is persistent (Freud). The dulling of sexuality is, apart from all else, inherent in satisfaction itself. It can only be delayed, not permanently eliminated, by varying the mode of satisfaction. But this physiologically based dulling differs from that caused by neurotic inhibition primarily because it is not the result of repression of drive demands but of satiety, and is therefore less painful. The later in life this dulling occurs, the more it will be simply a function of the natural decrease in efficiency of the sexual apparatus; no dangerous sexual stasis will take place. Complete awareness of the risks involved in too frequent intercourse is necessary so that voluntary abstinence will be practiced at times, even in marriage. Ferenczi (op. cit.) drew special attention to this. The close physical intimacy of marriage (common bedroom, etc.) makes this necessary abstinence difficult. If it is not practiced, husband and wife are one day confronted with the frightening fact of loss of sexual feeling, despite their previous sexual harmony. They then feel guilty and attempt to conceal the situation or compensate with exaggerated tenderness. Polygamous tendencies subsequently emerge and create confusion. The stronger the couple's ties to each other, the more intense the dismay, which may drive individuals to compulsive polygamous fantasies or acts. Due to the traditional view that marital infidelity is immoral, sinful, or criminal, severe guilt feelings develop. If adulterous tendencies remain an unexpressed "criminal" secret, if they are repressed, or if the spouse is deceived, neurotic illness becomes a threat, especially for a conscientious person. The less scrupulous person commits adultery and keeps it a secret. Very few have the courage to be candid with their partner; were such candor possible, it would have a liberating effect, even if it did not always overcome the difficulty. Temporary "infidelity" may even occasionally be desirable for a good marriage, but it presupposes complete awareness of the dangers that threaten the existence of the permanent relationship. On the other hand, it is very questionable whether fidelity based on compulsion or inhibition rather than on satisfaction is advantageous for a marriage. Certainly it is detrimental to psychic health.

In the light of these difficulties, the amount of marital unhappiness is no longer surprising, whether expressed in the murder of a spouse, in bitterness and quiet resignation, or as a neurosis. In marriage, sexual and economic interests always come into conflict with one another sooner or later, and since the bonds of tenderness grow with the length of the relationship whereas the sensual attraction wanes, a solution of the problem can be found only in a complete severance of sexual interests from economic ones.[9] One must be extremely wary of all prescriptions for marriage; the bleaker and more

[9] A detailed description may be found in "Sexual Maturity, Continence, Marital Morality" [in *The Sexual Revolution*. Reich considered the "exemplary sexual legislation" initiated in Soviet Russia during the early years of the Revolution to be an effort to implement such a severing of economic and sexual interests. (Ed.)].

disrupted the marital situation the more liberally they are handed out. They are attempts to salvage lost causes.

The Erotic and the Social Sense of Reality

The orgasm also exerts a decisive influence on the differentiated functions of the individual's social and cultural achievements. As Freud tells us, "even when we are considering the issue not of illness but rather of character formation, it is easy to see that sexual restriction is accompanied by a certain anxiousness and hesitation, whereas fearlessness and daring go hand in hand with sexual needs that are allowed free rein."[10] A comparison of the social and sexual achievements of those who are healthy and those who are ill demonstrates several typical relationships between primitive and highly developed functions, relationships that must not be overlooked when assessing the therapeutic task.

Pregenital drives are autoerotic by nature and thus asocial; the destructive drive and its erotic offspring, sadism, are antisocial. Forced into the social community, the individual must forfeit his actual drive goals and divert the corresponding energies to socially and culturally important goals, either for love of a cathected object or in obedience to the constraint exerted by education. Freud called this process "sublimation." One of the most important prerequisites for sublimation is that the diverted drive impulses not fall prey to repression, which prevents not only drive satisfaction but all other uses of the drive as well. In this sense the moral demands from which repression derives and the efforts toward social and cultural adjustment by which it is avoided are opposites. Repression

[10] A General Introduction to Psychoanalysis.

does occasionally promote social achievements similar to those produced by sublimation, but they are easily distinguishable from genuine sublimations by their reactive-exaggerated character and the forced impression they give. A further important difference is that a genuine social sense of reality is compatible with the erotic sense of reality and even presupposes it—as we shall have to prove. A false, compulsive-reactive sense of reality, on the other hand, does not tolerate the presence of the erotic sense of reality.

Among all drives, genitality alone can fulfill the function of the erotic sense of reality by virtue of the psychological, physiological, social, and biological conditions of life. The term "erotic sense of reality," which we owe to Ferenczi, is easy to justify. Psychologically, an impotent person feels inferior and is more or less unproductive in nonsexual areas as well. Physiologically, genital satisfaction is indicative of orgastic release of sexual tension and is thus one of the prerequisites for maintaining psychic equilibrium. In social terms, satisfied genitality, as the primary basis of a well-ordered psychic economy, is also the prerequisite for the ability to work, which is the only satisfaction-seeking tendency which society permits and, to some extent, condones. From the biological standpoint, genitality is the only one of all the drives that also serves the preservation of the species.

The fate of genital libido in abstinent individuals who appear to be psychically healthy still remains unclear. Although the degree of libidinal readiness and the rhythm of the need to release sexual tension certainly vary greatly from individual to individual, the somatic sexual apparatus has not ceased to function. Therefore, there being no manifestations of eunuchoidism, sexual tension must exist. It would be important to find out what outlet organically replenished sexuality finds when it is neither discharged through orgasm nor released in neurotic symptoms. Only on the basis of an analysis of people who remain healthy while living in total abstinence could we make any definite statements. Still, it would not be inaccurate to state that anyone who without the restriction of physical ailment lives continuously in abstinence is not obeying his conscious will but is subject to inhibitions or fixations. It is highly unlikely that a biological function as important as sexuality can be inhibited by anything except repression. It would be mere semantic juggling to ascribe such inhibition to a "hypofunction" of the somatic sexual apparatus, since, for example, eunuchs castrated after puberty retain their psychic sexual energy, and in normal persons, sexual energy may persist for some time after the climacteric. Admittedly, intense work and genuine sublimation may eliminate stasis, but in the light of our present knowledge of drive energy mechanisms, we cannot assume with certainty that this is possible on a permanent basis or beyond a certain limit. We prefer to leave the question open, since it is only theoretically relevant.

One thing can be said, however: *Healthy individuals, that is, people capable of working and loving, direct their genitality mainly toward sexual goals and their destructive drives and pregenital demands toward social and cultural ends. In pathological cases the situation is reversed: social achievement is sexualized and the destructive drive and pregenital drives dominate love life.*

Sexual Satisfaction and the Ability to Work

Here we shall discuss the *ability* to work, irrespective of the kind of work involved. The mechanisms of the psychic apparatus are determined by the interaction between various needs and tensions, on the one hand, and social influences on the other. The specific content and the form of the activity through which biological needs press for satisfaction are prescribed by both the immediate and the broad social situation. Therefore, if we are to grasp how the psychic apparatus operates, we must separate those needs that are anchored in physiological and biologically meaningful processes from those alterations, those quantitative and qualitative modifications of human basic needs, that are imposed by social existence.

"Pleasure in work" and "ability to work" are simply correlates of prevailing economic dynamics. "Pleasure in what work?" "Ability to work in which branch of social need?" These are questions of a purely social nature. The social situation—primarily the familial situation in which the individual develops—defines the particular contents that will engage existing tendencies. For instance, whether a strong destructive tendency finds satisfaction in the activities of a butcher, a soldier, or a surgeon is decided not by the specific characteristics of the tendency itself but by the economic, social, and familial circumstances in which this tendency evolves. The structure of the labor market is what is decisive. It decides whether a bent can come to fruition or not. Nor should it be forgotten that a member of the oppressed classes *must* obey these economic necessities rather than his individual inclination. Only among the upper bourgeoisie, and in certain circles of the intellectual petite bourgeoisie, is subjective inclination given a certain degree of free play.

Thus, whether the question of ability to work involves work in a factory, an office, or in a political party, the fundamental rules that determine the psychic structure "ability to work" (not to be confused with "pleasure in work") remain the same where identical social conditions prevail. Only *pleasure* in work will differ, depending on whether the economic necessity does or does not harmonize with the subjective inclination.

Given the present state of the capitalist economy and prevailing unemployment, the issue of the ability to work is of prime importance to workers and employees: their psychic apparatus must provide the working energy that the economic situation demands or they will go under. This issue is far removed from any question of inclination; the latter is hardly considered. But there is absolutely no doubt that here the healthy regulation of *sexual energy* is crucial.

For the sake of clarity, we must differentiate between sexual energy that can be sublimated and that which cannot. This differentiation is rather loose, inasmuch as the boundary line varies with individuals and even within the individual at different times. The amount of residue that cannot be sublimated and presses for immediate satisfaction is variable and depends on the nature of the individual's current psychic conflicts, economic situation, social position, and on too many additional factors to be contained in a generalization. Age, too, plays some part. Although the quantities of sexual energy that cannot be sublimated are indeterminate over any length of time, it can be stated that, qualitatively, this energy is chiefly genital energy. This is shown by the reciprocal relation between the individual's sexual activity and his social productivity.

1. *Low social productivity increases sexual excitation.* The statements of working men who are out of work, who have been condemned to long periods of inactivity, all bear each other out. During the time they are unemployed they suffered far more intensely from sexual excitation

than when they are working. When an individual is engaged in intense social activity, energy is withdrawn from sexual fantasies and ideas. Most sex hygienists have drawn the erroneous conclusion that intensive work enables one to give up sexual activity altogether. However, this is true only to a certain degree and only for a limited time, which varies from individual to individual. In fact, in the Clinic for Work Disturbances, the exact opposite was shown.

2. *Sexual satisfaction increases the ability to work.* This relation between gratification of unsublimated sexual energy and productive sublimation is not generally known but is surely the more significant issue. It is also not easily understood at first glance. An observation that can be made again and again is that one feels more or less unwilling to work after unsatisfying coitus, whereas joy in work suddenly increases after a satisfying sexual experience. The former phenomenon is, in view of what has already been said, easily understood: because sexuality is unsatisfied, interest remains chiefly attached to sexual ideas and hampers work. The latter phenomenon can be explained by the fact that, after satisfaction, sexual ideas lose their cathecting energy temporarily, so work is not disturbed by sexual tension.

But where does the increase in ability to work come from? Here we must inquire what has become of the sexual energy after satisfaction has been achieved. First it is transferred out of the state of tension into that of relaxation. Now what becomes of it? A typical observation provides the answer. From the purely phenomenological point of view, after a satisfying sexual experience, a heightened sense of self-confidence, a greater purposefulness, and a fuller sense of strength may be observed. In contrast to this, after an unsatisfying sexual experience, people remain oppressed by unease, restlessness, and diminished self-confidence. This permits the conclusion that, when sexual ideas have been satisfied, the free, unsublimated sexual energy is converted into narcissistic libido, that is, into a qualitatively different state. The heightened sense of strength and self-confidence results from this and is the reason for the increased productivity. Sexual satisfaction thus involves unburdening of the sexual apparatus and simultaneous strengthening of the system of sublimation.

In every sublimation three instinctual elements can be discerned:

1. Permanent diversion of destructive aggressiveness from object destruction (community consciousness, general interest in socially important achievements, social conscience, and social activity).
2. Permanent diversion of pregenital impulses from autoerotic goals (certain types of social activity, cultural interests, science, art, financial interests, ambition, etc.).
3. Unsublimated genital interest that maintains lasting, tender object relationships and alternates periodically with urges for orgastic discharge. Following release in the orgasm, it becomes attached to the existing sublimated tendencies.

Even though the psychoanalytic thesis that unused sexual energy is converted into work energy is correct, it involves an all-too-rigid and mechanistic view of energy conversion, if this is taken to mean a diminution of the quantum of sexual energy and a simultaneous increase in work capacity. Things are not as simple as that. Such a view would lead to the absurd conclusion that the more work there is to do, the greater must be the sexual restraint. It is easy to reach formulations such as this if the statement "civilization and culture grow at the expense of drive satisfaction" is taken in the abstract and mechanistically. Failure to differentiate between genital and pregenital sexuality leads to just this sort of mechanistic view of sublimation ("the less sexual activity, the greater the performance at work") and is largely the result of the biased sexual morality that continues to dominate the science of sexuality.

The relation of sexual satisfaction to work productivity is a dialectic one and, hence, must be formulated dialectically. To a certain degree, which will vary with the individual, limiting sexual activity will foster work productivity. Continued beyond a certain point, however, the process reverses itself. Interest can no longer be transformed, and the sexual energy that is neither converted nor satisfied but merely repressed, disturbs the ability to work. Free, periodically satisfied genitality is the precondition for an untroubled conversion of interest. Furthermore, it is important to note the following facts:

1. Nongenital energy is in great measure susceptible to sublimation; genital energy is so only to a very limited degree. But the susceptibility of even nongenital energy to sublimation is determined by the state of the genital energy.
2. When there is less energy cathecting nongenital drive goals, the capacity to sublimate increases; when there is more energy cathexis, this capacity is reduced.
3. Under conditions of high tension, genital energy shows a different relation to sublimation (disturbing) than that of energy under conditions that are relaxed and satisfied (fostering).

3. *In the long run, unsatisfied sexuality disturbs the ability to work.* Let us consider the situation of a person living in abstinence in whom significant amounts of sexual energy are taken up in social productivity. This means that cathecting energies are attached to nonsexual activities while the rest of the libido that cannot be sublimated is not utilized. This undischarged libido is in a state of tension, a fact that remains unimportant so long as the tension does not exceed certain limits. However, two notable phenomena prove that sexual tension rises constantly in spite of intensive work: first, there is increased restlessness and an intensification of conscious and unconscious sexual fantasies; second, there is an intensification of work activity that springs from an inner pressure rather than from external necessity. Social performance usually takes on a frantic quality; the person involved is unable to allow himself any rest. It is this state that renders his activity suspect. Analysis shows immediately that such people avoid rest because they are afraid of it; rest might lead to sexual fantasies.

This process of reactively drowning out sensual desire is progressive. For this reason, the "rage to work" constantly intensifies, until one day the compensation springs a leak. The process of decompensation, too, is progressive. Sexual stasis, which has finally become so great that it can no longer be invested in work, tears a hole in the compensation, and sexual energy begins to pour out, progressively enlarging the tear. But this disturbance does not occur without renewed efforts at compensation. The whole process may take weeks, months, or even years, but the end result is inevitable: neurotic work disturbance.[11]

[11] *Cf.* the section "Sublimation and Reaction Formation" in "The Genital and the Neurotic Character" [included in *Character Analysis* (New York: Farrar, Straus and Giroux, 1972).]

A sexual life in which the satisfaction of pregenital tendencies plays a greater part than genital primacy, is thus uneconomic and unsatisfying and will lead to the same result. In such cases there is an inhibition of genital object love and of the genital function (potency disturbance in men and a reduced or nonexistent capacity for genital experience in women), which reinforces the nongenital tendencies. This reinforcement, seen purely in terms of the economy of sexual energy, is detrimental; pregenital impulses create more sexual excitation than can be relieved through the satisfaction of these impulses alone. For instance, oral eroticism dominates the sexual life of many women, and kissing is more meaningful to them than sexual intercourse. Whereas this oral-erotic sexual activity will mobilize all free libido, simultaneous vaginal anesthesia will prevent satisfaction. This is true for all forms of sexual activity that do not ultimately culminate in the sexual act. To claim that everybody achieves sexual satisfaction in their own way is true only with regard to excitation in foreplay. Here, individuality has the broadest range. But final satisfaction is *by nature*, that is, physiologically, tied to the genital apparatus; only the genital apparatus can provide *orgastic* satisfaction.

In terms of the long-term ability to work, inadequate sexual satisfaction often leads to sexual repression and neurotic illness more quickly than does total abstinence when strong stimuli are present. Sexual fantasies are more conscious, more plentiful, and more disturbing, because the reactive compensation is less successful. But sometimes an individual frees himself of his tormenting sexual excitation by an act of repression, setting in motion the same mechanism that operates in the person who has lived in abstinence from the outset. His compensation through social achievement then becomes more successful.

Ability to work is not disturbed only by the direct impingement of sexual fantasies; energy is also withdrawn from the sublimating system in the following way. As we stated earlier, the energy expended on social achievement is derived primarily from pregenital and aggressive drives that have been deflected from their goals. If unsublimated libido is not allowed periodic satisfaction, it will first dam up and then stream into the pregenital and aggressive drives, intensifying them without enhancing the achievement. On the contrary, the sexual energy already invested in social achievements easily frees itself from the sublimation process when the original goals are revivified by the influx of unsublimated libido into their systems; in effect, the sublimation process and the corresponding infantile (pregenital) aims then start to compete with one another. Moreover, since the infantile demands become more insistent in proportion to the degree of deficiency of real sexual satisfaction, and since, furthermore, sublimations are socially imposed activities of the libido, it is obvious that the whole proud edifice of sublimations may easily crumble, as we can see in so many sudden acute work disturbances.

In conclusion, it must also be pointed out that different social achievements have different psychic or, as the case may be, narcissistic valences. It is clear that, as sublimations, scientific and artistic achievements have a high narcissistic-satisfaction value. No investigation has ever been undertaken to discern whether the work of a miner uses up more or less psychic energy than that of a scientist. But the narcissistic-gratification coefficient of the miner's work—assuming the same expenditure of energy—is certainly far below that of the scientist's. This can hardly be a matter of indifference in terms of libido economy. However, one cannot speak of "a miner's work" in general; since the issue of work achievement can never be detached from the existing social situation.

The Consequences for Therapy

No matter how much individual diversity there may be, a basic psychic structure exists and is expressed in certain drive constellations. This structure is related to its individual differences in a way analogous to that in which the structure we call a tree (oak, beech, etc.) is related to the differences in size and position of the branches of two different trees (oaks, beeches, etc.). Thus, there is no basis for the objection that "schematization," that is, the seeking of common traits, is not permissible in the psychic realm. The term "pathological" is used to indicate a distortion of the basic structure itself, not merely deviations from an otherwise normal basic structure.

Psychoanalytic therapy strives for a new ordering of drives in terms of the normal basic structure. In agreement with the conscious will of the patient, it stands firmly on the reality principle without judging attitudes as "good" or "bad"; it simply tries to discover which of the patient's attitudes correspond to the patient's own reality capability, and which disturb it. Through analytic clarification and the reliving of early conflicts—without any direct intervention—the drives automatically reorder themselves, allowing the latent, reality-adjusted basic structure, which had simply been buried, to emerge. Thus, as Freud demonstrated, analysis is simultaneously synthesis. It is in closer accord with the patient's nature than is education ("psychogogy") without analysis, because it neither promotes ideals or attempts to persuade.

Unquestionably, there is a goal in analytic therapy that

can be achieved apart from educational means: namely, *establishing the ability to work and to love;* to be more explicit, *the capacity for sexual gratification.* If after years of psychoanalytic practice, one can state that in no case— even where the elimination of repression was extensive— was there evidence of unbridled acting-out or a permanent intensification of existing instinctuality, this surely indicates that Freud's method, when practiced by qualified persons, is able to control the "explosive material" with which it works and that a well-regulated sex-economy ensures social adjustment. Patients who have been cured through psychoanalysis achieve both awareness of, and control over, their drives. This control is naturally no longer neurotic (paralyzing) but conscious (purposeful).

It is easy to demonstrate that the goal of establishing orgastic potency does not exceed the proper limits of medical jurisdiction. Naturally, we anticipate objections to the contrary and are glad to forestall them. The goal of restoring the ability to work is taken for granted, but I have come to believe that some analysts regard achievement of the full ability to love as a lesser self-evident goal. The reason for this bias is a readily understandable hesitation to clash with prevailing sexual morality.

The issue of personal self-determination, which psychoanalysis, in contrast to all other psychotherapeutic methods, believes must be protected, is settled for the great majority of patients from the very beginning. There is no question of intervention; they come to the physician expressly because of disturbances of genital functioning, or they soon recognize their impotence and want to be cured of it. Those who either compensate for their impotence or have a negative attitude toward sex due to a deep characterological peculiarity are in the minority. There are no exceptions to the rule that in analysis sex-negative patients will sooner or later encounter their genital demands. If the analysis has been conducted properly, the patient will acknowledge his desires and will himself recognize the significance of this inhibition of functioning. However, masturbational manipulations and fantasies, as well as modes of behavior during intercourse, must be discussed with the same thoroughness as the details of a compulsive ceremonial would be, for instance. To shrink from doing this, or to consider it an unnecessary intrusion to enlighten the patient at the correct moment about the processes during intercourse, is a sign of one's own inhibition, inherent in which is the obvious danger that the most important material for resolving the neurotic conflict and removing the sexual stasis will be neglected.

There is no denying that sublimation as a way out of neurosis is not as important for our patients as is generally assumed. Abreaction, too, is only a momentary, uncomprehensive means of resolving a conflict; furthermore, it can be considered therapeutically valuable only in the few cases of traumatic hysteria. Becoming conscious of unconscious conflicts is also merely a prerequisite for their resolution. Intellectual decisions, no matter how firm, are not sufficient to achieve a permanent restructuring of the drives, that is, a removal of the characterological reaction basis on which the neurosis rests. One part of this reaction basis, perhaps the most significant (because the most immediate), is stasis neurosis.

Through the systematic accumulation of catamneses, it has been confirmed that those patients who achieved a balanced sex life either during or shortly after treatment showed far greater stability in the improvement accomplished during analysis than did those who, because of lingering unresolved genital conflicts or external difficulties (milieu, age, physical defects, etc.), had not been fully freed of their sexual stasis.[12] The cases of symptom and character neuroses that tended to relapse are found among those who remained impotent or who, mainly for unresolved neurotic reasons, continued to live in abstinence.

Although the problem of the neurotic reaction basis is still essentially unsolved, it may be assumed with certainty that somatic libido stasis and a disposition toward anxiety are its principal elements. Unquestionably, liberation from fear of drive satisfaction is indispensable to achieving the therapeutic goal. And since fear of the supposed dangers of drive satisfaction produces sexual stasis, which in turn produces stasis anxiety and its symptoms, the course of cure in causal therapy, despite all individual variations in the neurotic process, indicates that removal of fear of drive satisfaction frees the drives from repression. Some drives are sublimated, whereas others press for satisfaction. With the removal of repression and the development of sublimations during analysis, the first part of the task, remission of symptoms, has been accomplished.

Numerous observations have shown that no analysis may be considered successful if the anxiety originally bound in the symptoms has not been set free. The process manifests itself in episodes of anxiety. Guilt feelings, too, must be retransformed into anxiety; only then is it possible to treat the sources of anxiety analytically. Among these, ego narcissism, the basis of castration anxiety, and sexual stasis, the source of stasis anxiety, are of primary importance. Since, as we have demonstrated earlier, aggression and yearning for the womb, or birth anxiety, depend on the intensity of sexual stasis and castration anxiety, they

[12] Cf. my paper "On Genitality: From the Standpoint of Psychoanalytic Prognosis and Therapy" [Early Writings, Vol. I (New York: Farrar, Straus and Giroux, 1975)].

play only a secondary role as anxiety sources. This may also be seen in the reaction to therapy, which varies with the elimination of each of the different anxiety sources.

With the successful analytic resolution of the neurosis, yearning for the womb and aggression are either given up, subordinated to other tendencies, or "sublimated." Genitality, on the other hand, retains its sexual goal relinquishing only its incestuous object. Why is it that here the automatic consequence of being freed of anxiety is an intensified striving toward the object, while there it is aversion from the previous aim? Usually, one quietly assumes that this will be the result of therapeutic success, without considering how the therapeutic process—namely freeing the patient from anxiety—can produce such different effects. However, this may not occur. Experience has confirmed the following exceptions:

1. Despite any amount of analytic insight, both yearning for the womb and destructive aggression are not relinquished (they remain refractory) as long as castration anxiety remains unanalyzed, or as long as partially liberated libido, after making a feeble advance to the genital position, flows back to the earlier fixation points (relapses).
2. There are cases which, without having been completely analyzed, remain permanently free of symptoms, the analysis having attacked and resolved the genital fixations *first*, before deeper fixations could complicate transference. Freed of castration anxiety, genital libido can automatically reduce the cathexis of other wishes.[13] The

[13] Permanent cures achieved by palliative psychotherapy are occasionally reported; their success was probably based on enabling the patient to overcome genital inhibitions. Spontaneous cures of hysteria—for instance, after marriage—can be explained in this way.

orgastic release of sexual stasis virtually eliminates the tendency to regress.

3. If the development of genital primacy is not fully completed during childhood, the "pull of the womb," that is, the inclination to pregenital gratification, predominates, despite the analysis of all anxiety sources.

Satisfied genital object love is thus the most powerful opponent of the destructive drive, of pregenital masochism, of yearning for the womb, and of the punitive super-ego. This superiority of sexuality over the destructive drive is the objective justification of our therapeutic efforts.

In this respect, analytic therapy encounters many insurmountable external difficulties that, in the most favorable cases, replace neurosis with real unhappiness; in unfavorable cases, they cause a relapse which one is powerless against because the external conditions cannot be altered. For instance, a woman driven by her masculine tendencies selects as her husband a feminine man (perhaps even one suffering from mild ejaculatio praecox) whom she can torment and dominate. If analysis is successful, if it brings about a transformation from masculinity to femininity and replaces clitoral eroticism with vaginal readiness, the woman, thus cured, is no longer able to accommodate herself to her inadequate husband; her new attitudes have awakened a desire for a strong, decisive man who is superior to her in all respects. Or she has become capable of achieving orgasm and awaits stimulation by her husband; he, however, is either sexually unknowledgeable or insufficiently potent. Furthermore, a marriage may have been contracted for neurotic reasons under highly unfavorable conditions and be indissoluble because of material circumstances. For this reason, the prognosis is better for patients who are unmarried or who, if married, are childless.

Solutions to such external difficulties are always uncertain. Occasionally, patients with special talents find escape in some kind of work, but their condition remains precarious and they are never completely able to cope with external demands. Sexual resignation always contains the danger of a relapse, since complete abstinence is not to be expected even of a person who was healthy to begin with, let alone a former neurotic who fell ill precisely because his sexual energy was too intense. Masturbational satisfaction may delay a relapse. However, if it is the sole means for satisfaction over a long period, it involves the same risk, because of fantasies and the incompleteness of psychic satisfaction, even if guilt and anxiety are totally absent. The only other alternative is infidelity. Here the influence of analysis ceases; the patient's ego ideal has assimilated drive-affirming elements during the analysis and is thus in a position to decide between marital fidelity, as dictated by prevailing morality, and the right to sexual fulfillment, which, in itself, is not immoral.

In retrospect, we must concede that our results are relatively insignificant in view of the sexual and socioeconomic misery of our times. Therapeutic work is limited from the outset because sexual satisfaction and sublimation, the only two valid remedies for neurosis and its equivalents, depend essentially on the socioeconomic milieu. The ability to withstand conflict without relapse is the second part of the analytic task and the ideal goal of causal psychoanalytic therapy; the analytic elimination of genital inhibitions and the liberation of drives to be sublimated are merely preparatory. Improved resistance to the difficulties of life can be achieved in almost all cases by competent analytic treatment. The rest of the immunizational work must be provided by real sexual satisfaction and by the patient's environment. Some patients, once they have been freed of their infantile familial ties, succeed either in improving their surroundings or in achieving a satisfying sexual life in defiance of social obligations. Others, however, are so heavily burdened by economic and social conditions that they are unable to rise above them and under this pressure finally settle for neurosis. Experience shows that the core of their difficulty is the real struggle against prevailing sexual regulations and its effects.

While we were dealing with the orgasm function and its relation to the neurotic process, the following important question awaited our attention: If the core of neurosis is a somatic process—that is, if the energy source for the symptoms and the neurotic character is a pathological, physical excitation process (sexual stasis)—and if a psychoanalytic cure of neurosis depends ultimately on changing or removing its somatic basis, should one not immediately attempt to cure this essentially organic disorder by organic means, rather than launch into the complex and protracted (because thorough) process of psychoanalysis? Are those people who accuse psychoanalysis of bias and who have faith only in somatic approaches, such as organotherapy, perhaps right after all?

We shall counter this question with a more lucid one: Is the family doctor who advises the mother of a hysterical girl to marry off her daughter immediately right or not? Is a neurologist correct to advise a man who is abstinent and neurotic to have intercourse? In principle, yes. Since dammed-up sexuality is the energy source of the pathological process, only its removal can effect a radical cure. In reality, however, the advice in both cases is bad. The girl will probably remain an hysterical and sexually fearful wife who will drive her husband and children into neurosis as well; and the abstinent young man will certainly prove impotent, otherwise he would long ago have taken the same course on his own. Both these people could regain their health by the measures recommended *if* they were psychically intact and able to allow normal sexual excitement free rein. Psychoanalysis makes possible a spontaneous organic "organotherapy," which functions, quantitatively and qualitatively from within, by bringing about the sublimation of certain sexual drives, by permitting social adjustments through transformation of destructiveness, and by removing unnecessary sexual inhibitions. The result: sexual satisfaction which removes sexual stasis. Even though disturbance of the genital function sustains neurosis by constantly supplying the neurotic process with dammed-up sexual energy (actual cause), the source of the disturbance itself is initially purely psychical (historical cause).

Let us assume that there really is a libido-heightening medication. If it were given to a neurotic who had no conscious sexual desire, the psychic inhibition barring excitation from the genitals would not decrease in the least. On the contrary, either the patient's neurotic anxiety would be intensified or the patient would develop new symptoms. And if there were a libido-diminishing medication, it would, of course, simultaneously allay anxiety. Certainly this would decrease the patient's neurotic reaction basis, although it would never eliminate it, and the entire psychic superstructure of his feeling of impotence would, at best, change only outwardly. His ability to sublimate would remain as weak as before because there would have been not qualitative changes—as there are after an analysis—but only a quantitative decrease of psychic energy. A nation that is obliged to support those who are unable to work would certainly object to such therapy.

Thus we see that even the most perfect organotherapy could not dispense with psychoanalysis, because the former can only add to or subtract from what is already there, whereas psychoanalysis influences energy distribution in the psychic apparatus. Only psychoanalysis, by bringing about changes in the ego, enables the psyche to allow qualitatively effective energy distribution and to sustain quantitative changes.

At present, however, all this is still utopian. Unfortunately, current research in the field of sexual chemistry remains partially in the realm of fantasy and partially in the dead end of emotional prejudice. On the other hand, the approach to the physiology of neurosis that psychoanalysis has indicated is taboo. Here, clearly, far more difficult issues are involved. Of crucial importance is the *prevention of neurosis* by eliminating the social factors that create neuroses en masse. This, however, leads to questions of the social regulation of sexual matters, of the position of the family in society, of pubertal and marital sex life, that is, to sociological and politico-cultural questions that do not belong within the framework of this book. Nevertheless, one can state with satisfaction that psychoanalytic research, with the sex-economy of neuroses as its point of departure, has crucial material to contribute to the sociological critique of our sexual mores.

Index

Abraham, K., 115
abstinence, neurotic, 116–18;
  based on ascetic ideology,
  121; motor unrest in, 169;
  voluntary in marriage, 198
actual neurosis, 9; Freud's
  theory of, 8
Adler, A., 38, 72, 173
aggression, definition of, 176; in
  the compulsive character,
  121; and pleasure, 175
aggression anxiety, *see* moral
  anxiety, 173ff.
amenorrhea, psychogenic, 113
amphimixis theory (Ferenczi),
  156
Andreas-Salomé, L., 166
angina pectoris, 80
anxiety, free-floating, 80, 89;
  freeing of, for analytic success, 214; and hysterical or
  compulsion-neurotic symptoms, 109; and sexuality, 82ff.
anxiety hysteria, 78, 109, 112
anxiety neurosis (Freud), 85–7
anxiety states, masturbation
  during, 84
arc de cercle, 112, 115
astasia-abasia, 115
asthenia (genital) in neurasthenia, 127ff.

asthma, and abstinence, 54
autonomic nervous system, and
  sexual excitation, 82ff.

Balzac, H. 188n., 190
Basedow's disease, 79, 80
Braun, 81, 82
Brissaud, 81

castration anxiety, 174
character formation and ego
  psychology, 4
Civilization and Its Discontents,
  36
climacteric, sexual activity in
  the, 171
coitus interruptus, 86
coitus, masturbational, curve of,
  50
compulsion neurosis, case of,
  120; erective impotence in,
  122; reaction to "genital
  danger" in, 121
compulsion neurotics, aggression
  in, 121, 177; ejaculation in,
  123; guilt feelings in, 175
compulsive vs. hysterical
  characters, 119
conversion symptoms, evidence
  of, in non-genital regions,
  113ff.; exclusion of the genitals
  in, 113; sexual energy in, 112

221

The works of Wilhelm Reich are published in cooperation with The Wilhelm Reich Infant Trust Fund. Those seeking additional information are advised to contact the trust fund at 382 Burns Street, Forest Hills, N.Y. 11375, or The Wilhelm Reich Museum, Orgonon, Rangeley, Maine 04970.